GOD'S POWER

for

PROTECTION

GOD'S POWER

for

PROTECTION

Melanie Hemry & Gina Lynnes

WHITAKER
HOUSE

Unless otherwise indicated, all Scripture quotations are taken from the *New King James Version*, © 1979, 1980, 1982, 1984 by Thomas Nelson, Inc. Used by permission. All rights reserved. Scripture quotation marked (AMP) is taken from the *Amplified® Bible*, © 1954, 1958, 1962, 1964, 1965, 1987 by The Lockman Foundation. Used by permission. (www.Lockman.org). Scripture quotations marked (NASB) are taken from the updated *New American Standard Bible®*, NASB®, © 1960, 1962, 1963, 1968, 1971, 1972, 1973, 1975, 1977, 1995 by The Lockman Foundation. Used by permission. (www.Lockman.org).

GOD'S POWER FOR PROTECTION

(Previously published as *Anointing for Protection*)

ISBN: 978-1-60374-924-4
eBook ISBN: 978-1-60374-925-1
Printed in the United States of America
© 2007, 2013 by Melanie Hemry and Gina Lynnes

Whitaker House
1030 Hunt Valley Circle
New Kensington, PA 15068
www.whitakerhouse.com

Library of Congress Cataloging-in-Publication Data (Pending)

1 2 3 4 5 6 7 8 9 10 11   20 19 18 17 16 15 14 13

CONTENTS

Part One

FEAR NOT. ONLY BELIEVE.

By Gina

Part One

FEAR NOT. ONLY BELIEVE.

*The thing I greatly feared has come upon me, and what I
dreaded has happened to me.*
—Job 3:25

*As soon as Jesus heard the word that was spoken, He said to
the ruler of the synagogue, "Do not be afraid; only believe."*
—Mark 5:36

We live in a dangerous world—a world that, try as it may,
cannot promise us protection. I first found that out when, as a
sleeping twelve-year-old girl, I heard the devil's wart-encrusted
hand of fear rake its jagged fingernails across my window screen.

The *scritching* sound of a sharp edge brushing across wire mesh
is what woke me. Not that my slumber had been deep anyway. I'd

perched for hours on the edge of unconsciousness, gathering the guts to jump. Squeezing my eyelids tight against the darkness of my bedroom, I had dared myself to go to sleep…even though my parents were gone…and the house was empty…and I was alone late at night for the first time.

As an almost-teenager, I was plenty old enough to take care of myself. Or so I had assured my mother and father. I believed it, too, early in the evening when the sun glowed through the drapes in my room, making warm rectangles of light on the carpet. I believed it as I pushed those drapes aside and gazed over the boxwood hedge that bordered my window as my parents' massive green Ford lumbered down the street and disappeared, not to return until the wee hours of the morning.

"What could possibly happen to a young girl nestled safe in her bed behind locked doors in an ordinary suburban neighborhood?" I had asked them (and myself) as they fussed over me before they left. "*What harm could possibly come?*"

Granted, in years past, I harbored silly kindergarten fears that sent me diving under beds or quivering beneath piles of laundry when I found myself at home alone for even a few measly minutes. But I'd outgrown those terrors and tossed them out with my Laddie pencils and Big Chief tablets. I looked back with disdain on the days when every creak in an empty house morphed into the footstep of some black-eyed, craggy-faced killer coming after me to…

Well, I didn't really know what he was coming after me for… but whatever it was had once made my seven-year-old heart thrash in my chest and thunder in my ears. It had made my mouth go dry as a west Texas dust storm and my throat tighten up like a hangman's noose.

If I had forgotten what that kind of fear felt like as I turned off the bedside lamp that night and prepared to sleep alone in an empty house for the first time, the memory came rushing back a few hours later when my eyes bugged open at the sound of fingernails on my window screen. My ears tingled as the noise echoed against my eardrums. *What was that?* I pressed my head into the softness of my pillow, resisting the iron grip of fear that threatened to clamp around my mind.

One little scrape. Come on, get a grip. It was one little sound. It was nothing, I chanted to myself in silence. The noise stopped. *See? Nothing at all.*

Drawing a deep breath, I commanded myself to relax and close my eyes.

The snap of a boxwood branch forced them open again. On the other side of the floor-to-ceiling window across the room, shadows danced to the shooshing of leaves awakened from their slumber on a windless night.

Scritch. There it was again, followed by a click and the sound of the window screen shifting in its place.

Was it that? Or my imagination?

The boxwood hedge shook again, this time not just wakened but alarmed; it flailed its leafy arms and grazed the window in excitement. Unable to hold the tension any longer, my coiled muscles sprang loose, catapulting me from my bed. I didn't care how grown up I was. I didn't care if I was laughed out of the neighborhood. I raced barefooted and breathless to the phone. Across the street, porch lights blinked on as our neighbor, a former professional football player and family friend, came striding across his lawn, flashlight in hand, to my rescue.

I cringed, gnawing on my knuckles at the doorway of my bedroom as the beam of his flashlight flickered and darted through the filter of my bedroom curtains. Pinpricks of alarm stabbed at the back of my neck as I listened to the sound of his bulky frame breaking through the shrubs—the same sound I'd heard earlier. Even so, when I opened the front door to thank him for his help, I expected him to tousle my hair and tell me it was nothing. To go back to sleep. That my parents would be home soon and there was nothing to worry about.

Instead, he stood at our front door frowning and shaking his head, his massive barrel shape backlit by the moonlight. "I don't know," he said. "Maybe it was just an animal. But I think it would be best if you came over to our house until your folks get home. Just to be on the safe side."

The safe side?

My kind neighbor didn't realize at that moment—even I didn't realize—that it was too late for me to be on the safe side. The devil's finger had already furrowed my heart with an open wound of fear and filled it with seeds of terror. He had reached out when no one was looking and planted them there to hide in darkness until he, as the prince of darkness, decided the time was right for them to yield their harvest of destruction.

That night as I padded across the street, a frowsy-headed twelve-year-old girl in house shoes and a bathrobe, to take refuge in my neighbor's house, I was taking my first few steps toward what Job once called, *"that which I greatly fear."* Unless God Himself intervened and arrested the process I would never be on the safe side again.

Riding in on Vulture's Wings

"Fear not!" It's easy to find those words in the Bible. They appear so often that God might well have added, "If I've said it once, I've said it a hundred times. *Fear not!*" Yet most of us—even those of us who know the Word of God well—don't take that command seriously. To be honest, we don't consider it a command at all. We view it more like a good, but impractical, suggestion. We often disregard it without a thought because we don't recognize the deadly potential of the devil's seeds of fear that crop up like weeds in our lives.

I must admit, I didn't consider it a command. If I had, I would have responded in a different way to the little sprouts of terror that began to bud in my heart after that scary night. I would have slapped on my spiritual gardening gloves, grabbed the spade of God's Word, and dug up the filthy things. But I didn't. Instead, I did what most people do. I ignored them and hoped that as the chilling memory of the incident faded, the fear would vanish along with it.

When thoughts of it slithered up from the depths of my subconscious on occasion and hissed at me, I whacked at them with the hoe of reason. *What are the odds?* I'd ask myself with the logic I inherited from my accountant mother and my engineer father. *What is the likelihood that such a thing would happen to the same person twice?* No, I'd had my brush with danger and escaped unharmed. It was ridiculous to imagine it could happen again.

Sure enough, the years ticked by with no recurrence. One… two…three…four… Granted, I rarely stayed alone at night. Five… six…seven…eight. And when I did, I left lights burning from dusk till dawn just in case. Nine…ten. But those were just precautions any reasonable person would take—precautions that were wholly unnecessary. At least, that's what I told myself. I believed it, too, until ten years after the thorny weeds of fear were planted, they ripened and proved me wrong.

Looking back now, what happened that night makes perfect sense. It was as predictable as gravity. What goes up must come down. The forces of nature demand it. Whatever we greatly fear will, in some form, come upon us. The devil himself will see to that. He rides into our lives on vulture's wings of fear, just as God moves in our lives on eagle's wings of faith.

That fact shouldn't surprise us. After all, the devil learned everything he knows from watching God.

Back in the days when he was the anointed cherub on heaven's mountain, back in the time when he *"walked up and down in the midst of the stones of fire"* (Ezekiel 28:14 KJV) before iniquity was found in him, the devil studied God's ways. (See verses 13–16.) He figured out that the divine law of faith is incontrovertible. When God's creatures believe His Word, that Word comes to pass for them. The proclamation Jesus made to the centurion holds true for all: *"as you have believed, so let it be done for you"* (Matthew 8:13). Nobody knows that better than the devil himself.

It's no wonder, then, that in his battle against God's children, Satan employs the same strategy—with a malicious twist. He poisons our minds with his own wicked words. He whispers to us threats of death and destruction. He arranges circumstances to confirm the validity of those threats. Then he backs them up with evil reports and blood-curdling emotions until we believe what he has told us.

Once we believe him, we're easy prey.

I didn't understand that strategy the night the devil decided after ten dormant years that it was time to fulfill my fears. By that time, I'd accepted them as part of my life. As much as possible, I kept them shoved in a corner and forced myself to be brave. I had no choice. A failed marriage had left me to manage alone in a ramshackle duplex with my infant son. So, night after night, as I struggled to drift off to sleep, squeezing my eyelids shut like I did as a little girl, I told myself there was really nothing to fear.

I didn't believe it, though. I knew there was a great deal to fear in this sin-racked, demon-infested world. My only comfort came from the memory that sometimes neighbors can come to your rescue—and on the other side of the center wall of my duplex lived a very good neighbor. He was a clean-cut young man who had assured me the day I moved into the place that if I ever needed help I could just rap on the wall and he'd come running.

My neighbor was out of town the night the rattling at my front door jarred me awake.

The hollow clicking of metal against metal is what first roused my sleepy mind. My eyes jerked open as I recognized the sound, and I caught my breath as if I'd been doused with a bucket of icy water. As a frigid surge shot through me, I pleaded for my pounding heart to be silent so I could hear the noises of the house.

For a few blessed moments, it seemed the clicking had stopped. I lay still as a dead man under the shroud of my bed sheets and listened to be sure.

Seconds passed and I inhaled, forcing my ribcage to expand despite the fear that constricted it. I told myself I'd been dreaming...or perhaps I was just hearing the normal creaks and pops characteristic of old houses. *Yes, that's what it was.* I let out my breath in a slow, silent stream, relieved to hear only the soft sighs and murmurs of my son sleeping in his crib a few feet from my bed. The familiar ticking of the alarm clock on my nightstand reassured me. Its hands pointed at a jaunty 45-degree angle. *Three o'clock and all's well*, it seemed to say.

Silly me. Pulling the blanket snug around my chin, I rolled over in defiance and turned my back to the bedroom door where the light streamed in from the living room lamp I left burning every night.

Then I heard the rattle again.

I knew this time it was real. The sound was unmistakable. Someone was picking the lock on my front door.

In a single moment, the paper-thin barriers of false confidence I'd erected over the years to keep my terror at bay collapsed. A flood of horror swept every coherent thought from my mind. Every thought except one: *my neighbor said he would help!*

Stealing from my bed, I moved toward our adjoining wall. I knotted my fist and raised it in the shadows to sound the alarm that would rouse him to my rescue.

Then it hit me. He was gone. No one would come.

The relentless racket at the front door continued. I fastened my eyes on my sleeping baby and the tide of panic rose higher. I had to do something. For my baby's sake, if nothing else.

The police! I need to call the police! But what if the intruder gets in before they arrive? What if they're too late?

I went rigid at the thought. Then logic kicked in again. Maybe I was just imagining things after all. How foolish I'd feel if the police came and found a stray cat on my porch, or a dog scratching against the door. Be a big girl. Check it out.

I crept toward the front door, my whole body vibrating to the rhythm of my racing heart, my breath sucked from me by the vampire of fear. Stepping into the pathway of lamplight that spilled from the living room, my eyes fixed in horror on the doorknob. It rotated back and forth, rattling as it moved.

The lock hadn't yet given way, but it couldn't last much longer.

I stood transfixed and watched unblinking as the knob turned again. The black-eyed, craggy-faced villain of my childhood had finally caught up with me. I could no longer hide.

CALL THE POLICE!

The command erupted from somewhere inside me with a shout that freed me from my trance and sent me stumbling toward the phone. The intruder must have known by then I was awake. He must have heard me bumping around. He also must have known I was alone because he didn't flee. Instead he jimmied the lock with greater vigor, determined to break in before anyone could stop him.

I have no memory of making the call. I just know I did it. What I remember is the torturous minutes that passed as I waited for the police to arrive.

I could have spent those minutes praying for God to help me, but I didn't. It never occurred to me. I had developed such a stronghold of fear that it seemed even God couldn't deliver me from the hand of this evil.

I could have grabbed a skillet or a fireplace poker and prepared to fight, but I didn't do that, either. Instead, I did what the devil had been preparing me to do for ten years. I stood like a helpless victim waiting to experience my greatest fear.

Edging to the door, I peered through the peephole to see my attacker. Sure enough, he was there, crouching bare-chested on my front porch and fiddling with the lock. The half-light that filtered from the street lamp through the swaying branches of the elm in my front yard snaked shadows across his back. He was racing the arrival of the police—whether he knew it or not—and it seemed likely he would win.

Someone else was praying for me that night. I don't know who, and I don't know where. But I'm confident someone was, because several minutes before the police car pulled to the curb at the end of my sidewalk, its headlights beaming through my flimsy window shades, the intruder jumped as though he'd seen a ghost and high-tailed it around the corner of the house. Astounded, I listened to his footsteps echo across the porch boards, thump into the garden soil below, and fade away.

The policeman who arrived at my door a few minutes later scribbled the details of my story on a notepad and examined the scrapes around the lock. "Anything else I can do for you, ma'am?" he asked, looking down at me from beneath the brim of his cap. "You gonna to be all right now?"

"Sure, I'll be fine," I lied.

As he turned to go, I blurted out the question I'd been living with for years.

"Do you think he'll come back?"

"No, ma'am. I don't expect he'd do that. He probably knows we're onto him now."

"Of course he does," I said, forcing a smile. "Good night, officer."

"Good night, ma'am."

That same night, a few blocks west of my house, another woman didn't wake up in time to call the police. Or maybe her door lock was more cooperative than mine. Or maybe nobody was praying for her. For whatever reason, she suffered what I was spared.

Although his crime was not averted, the criminal was apprehended that night. The drugs he'd taken overtook him, and he passed out at the scene of the crime. Judging from what I heard on the news, the case against him was cut-and-dried. I assume he ended up behind bars. But in my mind, he—or someone like him—would be forever prowling the streets.

Someday he would find me again. I was sure of it.

Rescued by the Prince of Peace

Over the next few years, I searched for some sense of security that could free me from the fear that stalked me every night I was alone. I'd never heard about God's promises of protection even though I'd gone to church all my life. Sure, I'd heard the Bible stories in Sunday school. I'd spent years sitting alongside my tiny denominational peers, fidgeting in diminutive wooden chairs as the teachers told us how God saved David from Goliath, how He kept the lions from turning Daniel into a bedtime snack, or how He kept Shadrach, Meshach, and *To-Bed-You-Go* from roasting in the hottest furnace of all time.

They were interesting stories, but I didn't find much comfort in them because the moral (*God is powerful enough to deliver His children from any danger and keep them safe*) had a monster catch attached to them. The catch was this: *Although God always has power to protect His children, sometimes He just doesn't do it.* "God works in mysterious ways," our devoted teachers warned as they peered with somber eyes over the edges of their massive Bibles. "You never know what God is going to do."

Great. That's reassuring.

When I grew old enough and bold enough to inquire why God might want to leave His obedient children squirming in the jaws of calamity, why He might choose to let some sweet saint be slashed to pieces in a car wreck, or slung from the sky in a malfunctioning plane, or preyed upon by violence of some other kind, my queries were discouraged. "We don't question God," I was told. "He loves us. He is our best Friend and always does for us what is best, no matter how terrible that thing might seem to be at the time."

I never said it, but I thought it: *With friends like that, who needs enemies?*

It's no surprise, then, that when my fears exploded into phobias, the last place I thought to look for help was the Bible. I turned instead to a therapist, someone in whom I could confide the full extent of my raging terror. Someone who, even if he thought I was as nutty as a pecan tree, couldn't spread the news to my friends and family. Someone who had the professional training necessary to make me feel safe again.

Week after week, I sat in his office and dumped my paranoia into his capable hands so that he could sort through it and straighten things out. I told him about the incidents that sparked my fears. I confessed that even though years had passed since I discovered the intruder at my door, and even though I now had three children to make me feel less alone, my terrors consumed me on nights when my husband was out of town. They shook me until my teeth chattered. They squeezed me with a python grip until I couldn't breathe. They shot chemicals through my bloodstream until a clammy film of perspiration made the bedclothes cling to me like a mummy's wrap.

I confessed with shame that, under the influence of my fears, a cloud creeping across a full moon and casting a shadow on the window convinced me a leering intruder stood outside. The click of the refrigerator compressor in the darkened kitchen became the sound of a killer opening the back door. The sense that someone evil had slipped into the house under cover of night became so palpable that at times I stared unblinking into the blackness until my eyes watered from straining to see who was there.

Of course, I didn't even tell my therapist everything. I didn't tell him, for instance, that I fortified myself against any possible attack by keeping a sawed-off shotgun under the edge of the bed within arm's reach. Later, a 357 Magnum was hidden in the nightstand. Nobody but my husband knew they were there.

It was crazy. What's worse, in the light of day, I knew it was crazy. But at night when no one was there to protect me, it was my reality.

In the seventies, doctors and therapists weren't as quick to medicate emotions as they are today. If they had been, I'm sure

I would have ended up with a medicine cabinet full of pills to comfort me. I would have used chemicals to bind and gag my terrified mind so that it couldn't scream at me anymore. The fears still would have been there, of course, but the drugs would have muffled their cries.

As it was, I was on my own. Therapy didn't help. I did find blessed relief, though, when my husband's job stopped taking him out of town for a while and I no longer spent nights alone. With him there to protect me as I drifted off to sleep, the shadows and sounds in the darkness stopped frightening me. Months went by without terror. I put the guns in storage. I was finally all right.

Then we moved to another state. My husband started to travel, and the nightmare began again.

This time, however, something was different.

I was different.

During the previous two years, I'd dedicated my life to Jesus Christ and made Him my Lord. I'd received the baptism of the Holy Spirit. I'd gone to work for a Christian ministry. And, most important of all, I'd discovered the power of God's written Word.

By the time I faced my old fears again, I'd already learned to use that Word to drive sickness out of my body. I'd discovered how to swing it like a sword to separate myself from sinful habits that had dogged me for years. So I almost popped my cork the day I settled into my seat at a believers' meeting, pen and paper in hand, ready to take notes, and heard the speaker say, "Open your Bibles, please, to Psalm 91. Today we're going to talk about God's promises of protection."

God's promises of protection. Those were some of the sweetest words I'd ever heard. I'd been taught for years about God's *power* for protection. I knew about the *possibility* of God's protection. But God's *promise* of protection was something else altogether.

The promises in God's Word are His guarantee. They are His unbreakable bond. Once He makes them, He keeps them without fail because it is impossible for Him to lie. If God had promised in His Word to protect me and I dared to believe those promises, I could live in safety no matter how many criminals prowled the streets.

My mind reeled as people around me rustled through the pages of their Bibles. The chill of the air-conditioned breeze that wafted across the convention center raised goose bumps on my arms and sent a shiver of anticipation down my spine. *If God has promised to protect me, I can spit in the eye of every terror that has tormented me. I never have to live in fear again.* The amplified echo of the preacher's voice beginning to read set me fumbling with desperate fingers to find Psalm 91 in time to follow along. I didn't want to miss a word.

> *He who dwells in the secret place of the Most High shall abide under the shadow of the Almighty. I will say of the LORD, "He is my refuge and my fortress; My God, in Him I will trust." Surely He shall deliver you from the snare of the fowler and from the perilous pestilence. He shall cover you with His feathers, and under His wings you shall take refuge; His truth shall be your shield and buckler. You shall not be afraid of the terror by night, nor of the arrow that flies by day, nor of the pestilence that walks in darkness, nor of the destruction that lays waste at noonday.*   (Psalm 91:1–6)

I flashed back on a hundred sleepless nights spent shaking in the grip of fear. *"You shall not be afraid of the terror by night."*

I remembered how alone I felt, how vulnerable and unprotected. *"He shall cover you with His feathers, and under His wings you shall take refuge."*

I thought of the shotgun beneath my bed and the handgun in my nightstand. *"His truth shall be your shield and buckler."*

Tearful waves of relief surged up from my heart and threatened to spill over the levee of my eyelids as I read on. In the background, the speaker's voice echoed across the auditorium, but I'd lost track of her message. I was suddenly lost in what seemed like a spiritual fairy tale all my own. Like the fabled princess Rapunzel, I'd been trapped alone in a tower of nighttime terror since I was twelve years old. I'd hoped for decades to be rescued. Now, at last, my Prince of Peace had come to set me free.

As my eyes searched the next words of the psalm, the Holy Spirit prefaced each one with my name. He whispered the phrases to my heart as if each one had been written just for me.

> *Because you have made the LORD, who is my refuge, even the Most High, your dwelling place, no evil shall befall you, nor shall any plague come near your dwelling; for He shall give His angels charge over you, to keep you in all your ways. In their hands they shall bear you up, lest you dash your foot against a stone. You shall tread upon the lion and the cobra, the young lion and the serpent you shall trample underfoot.*
>
> (Psalm 91:9–13)

The levee burst, and salty waves cascaded down my cheeks and onto the crinkling pages of my Bible. Not only had my Prince come, but He'd brought the armies of heaven with Him! He'd commanded the angelic hosts to surround me and keep me safe. He'd charged them to make sure nothing hurt me.

I recalled the serpentine fears that had wound themselves around me in the darkness until I gasped for air and realized for the first time that their power had been stripped from them. My shoulders straightened and my head snapped up in triumph at the thought. *I will tread upon those serpents and trample them underfoot.*

Fishing a tissue from my purse, I blotted at the tiny pools of tears that magnified various letters and words of Psalm 91 as they shimmered on the pages of my open Bible. Around me, I heard people turning pages again. The speaker had started teaching from other passages of Scripture. I wasn't yet ready to move on. Still awed by Psalm 91, I let the last three verses wash over me with the tenderness of a love song.

> *Because he has set his love upon Me, therefore I will deliver him; I will set him on high, because he has known My name. He shall call upon Me, and I will answer him; I will be with him in trouble; I will deliver him and honor him. With long life I will satisfy him, and show him My salvation.*
>
> (Psalm 91:14–16)

My love had been set on Jesus long before I walked into the meeting that day. There was no question in my mind about it. But surrounded by the protective embrace of these precious promises, I was swept off my feet by a torrent of fresh affection for Him. Overwhelmed with gratitude, I wanted to hug my Bible and kiss its grainy, cowhide cover.

My Lord Jesus had just crushed my greatest fear under the mighty heel of His Word. Using my open Bible, He had over-turned the religious theories that left open the possibility that God might want my life to be wrecked by calamity or snuffed out early by some disaster. He had cleansed my mind of the nagging questions about His willingness to protect me. He had assured me once and for all that He had committed Himself to defend me against the Goliaths in my life, to shut the mouth of every hungry lion that leered at me with drooling chops, to walk with me through every fiery circumstance and bring me out unharmed and smelling like a rose.

If I would do my part by dwelling in His secret place and speaking words of faith, He would surely do His part by keeping me and my family safe even in the most dangerous times. I knew that now and I determined never to doubt it again.

A gentle tap on my shoulder roused me from my revelatory reverie.

"Excuse me."

I looked up to see another believer standing beside me, dangling his car keys in one hand and gripping his Bible in the other, waiting for me to vacate my chair so he could get to the aisle and go home. The murmur of chattering saints gathering their belongings and milling toward the door registered on my ears. The meeting was over. I had missed most of speaker's message. But I'd heard every word the Lord had spoken to my heart.

I closed my Bible and slung my purse over my shoulder.

I'd never be the same again.

Passing the Test

I walked out of that meeting knowing full well that the devil had been brainwashing me for years. That was the plain truth. I'd spent thousands of hours being harassed by the terrifying images he projected into my thoughts. And I was smart enough to know that it would take more than one reading of Psalm 91 to free me of them.

Although God had promised to protect me, I knew I had to develop faith to stand on that promise. I had to wash my mind with the water of His Word until the muck left behind by years of fearful thinking was rinsed away. *"If you abide in My word, you are My disciples indeed,"* Jesus said. *"And you shall know the truth, and the truth shall make you free"* (John 8:31–32). To be free, I had to keep the truth about God's promise of protection in my mind and in my mouth until I lived in that truth and it lived in me. So I buckled down and went after it.

I read Psalm 91 and other Scriptures like it first thing in the morning and before bed at night. I talked to God about them every day, thanking Him and rejoicing with Him over His protection. I made up little songs about it and sang them while I loaded the dishwasher and dusted the furniture.

As the days passed, I sensed a lightness in my heart I hadn't experienced since childhood. I felt like I'd climbed into the basket of a hot air balloon, cast aside the sandbags of fear, and been borne aloft by the wind of the Holy Spirit. At last, instead of slogging through the darkness and dangers of the world, I was floating above them in the endless sky of God's love.

Pleasant as that was, however, I knew that every revelation from God's Word will be tested by adverse circumstances. Until we have passed such a test, we cannot be sure we truly believe that Word.

The night I faced my test, the circumstances were all too familiar.

My husband was out of town, and I was alone in the house with the children. I had outgrown the need to leave a light on all night, so the house was swathed in darkness. The metal cookie sheets I'd once propped against the doors so they would topple and clatter to warn me of incoming intruders were gone, returned to the kitchen cabinets where they belonged.

Who needs cookie sheets crashing around in the middle of the night when there are angels guarding every door?

Others might scoff, but I had no doubt the angels were there—camping out on my front porch, standing guard in the backyard at the sliding glass door by the patio, and keeping watch at the laundry room door that adjoined the garage. After I understood the promise in Psalm 91, I'd asked God to send those angels. I thanked God for their presence most nights before I went to sleep.

As a result, my slumber was no longer fitful but deep and sound. I didn't just doze anymore. I hibernated, no more expecting to be attacked, or even awakened, than a bear snoozing the winter away in his cave.

So when my eyes flew open to the familiar metallic rattle of doorknob jiggling against the lock, it took me a moment to process the sound.

In an instant, all the old sensations of terror came flooding back. My muscles went rigid. A trap door slammed shut in the back of my throat and cut my breath short. Goose bumps climbed one atop the other like pyramiding cheerleaders at a football game.

I laid in the dark and listened with all my might.

Nothing.

Had I really heard anything after all? Was it just a dream…or the old imaginations coming back?

I wasn't sure.

My heart thumping, I considered tiptoeing down the hallway toward the door to investigate. I trembled at the memory of the last time I'd made that trip. I saw again the shadowy shape that had crouched on the other side of the door. *Would I ever escape that memory?*

As if in answer, the words of the psalm arose from my spirit and pierced through the clamor of my mind.

I will say of the Lord, "He is my refuge and my fortress; my God, in Him I will trust."…He shall cover you with His feathers, and under His wings you shall take refuge; His truth shall be your shield and buckler. You shall not be afraid of the terror by night. (Psalm 91:2, 4–5)

If I ever had any doubt that the Word of God is alive, it was settled that night when Psalm 91 came marching up out of my heart where I'd hidden it. Verse after verse stormed onto the shores of my consciousness. Their presence was more real than any flesh-and-blood defender could ever be.

Reinforced by the promises of God's protection, I exchanged terror for righteous anger. Throwing back the blanket I'd pulled up to my eyes, I opened my mouth, swung the Sword of the Spirit, and put my true attacker on the run.

"You listen to me, Satan, and you listen good. Because I have made the Lord my refuge, and the Most High my dwelling place, no evil shall befall me, nor shall any plague come near my dwelling. God has given His angels charge over me to keep me in all my ways. They're protecting me tonight, and I know it. So you take your stupid fears and get out of here. I'm going back to sleep."

And that's what I did. I fluffed my pillow, settled my head in its puffy embrace, and relaxed in the secret place of the Most High, feeling sorry for any poor fool who tried to tangle with the angels looming outside my doors. I was aware, even as I dozed off, that the house was quiet. No more strange noises. *Oh well, it probably wasn't anything after all*, I thought as I sank into a peaceful sleep.

When the phone rang me awake, the house was still dark.

Who would be calling at this hour?

Backhanding the sleep from my eyes, I struggled to shake the cobwebs from my brain, then flung my arm across the bed and groped at the nightstand until I found the telephone.

"Hello?" I croaked.

"Hello. This is the Edmond Police Department."

I shot up from the bed, wide awake in a split second. "The police?"

"Yes, ma'am. An officer cruising your area asked us to notify you that your garage door is open and to make sure that everything is all right there."

Whether I left the garage door open that night or someone else opened it, I still don't know. But I do know this: nobody was able to get in because I have some mighty big angels stationed around my house. And it seems that, when necessary, they know how to contact the police.

I padded across the house to close the door, a frowsy-headed child of God wrapped in a housecoat and swaddled in a peace that passed understanding. Smiling, I recalled the frightening night so many years before when I was twelve years old and my kind neighbor tried to lead me to the safe side.

Thank God, I had finally arrived.

Fewer Dropped Calls

Over the next few months, I learned more about God's promises of protection. I discovered, for instance, that it works best when we stay in communication with Him. I also found that hearing from the God of heaven while we're stuck here on the earth is much like talking to someone on a cell phone. The conversation goes well if we stay within range of His signal. As long as we can hear His voice, we have nothing to worry about. He can warn us of impending danger and lead around it. He can instruct us in the way that we should go. So we can say with the boldness of David:

The LORD is my light and my salvation; whom shall I fear? The LORD is the strength of my life; of whom shall I be afraid? When the wicked came against me to eat up my flesh, my enemies and foes, they stumbled and fell. Though an army may encamp against me, my heart shall not fear; though war

*should rise against me, in this I will be confident. One thing
I have desired of the LORD, that will I seek: that I may dwell
in the house of the LORD all the days of my life, to behold the
beauty of the LORD, and to inquire in His temple. For in the
time of trouble He shall hide me in His pavilion; in the secret
place of His tabernacle He shall hide me; He shall set me high
upon a rock. And now my head shall be lifted up above my
enemies all around me.*   (Psalm 27:1–6)

Hiding in "the pavilion" of the Lord, as that passage calls it, or
"dwelling in the secret place of the Most High," as Psalm 91 calls
it, is like being in a geographical location where your cell phone
signal is strong. When you get a call, it's easy to hear and understand the caller. Outside the secret place, you run into trouble. The
signal starts breaking up. Sometimes the call gets dropped.

When it comes to living in God's protection in dangerous days
like these, what we want is fewer dropped calls.

When I first discovered that secret place of protection, I didn't
know much about cell phones. Back then, all my telephones were
still tethered to the wall. But I figured that to maintain my wireless
communication with God, I need three basic elements.

The first is faith. To hear the voice of the Lord and be hooked
up with Him in any area of life, I must believe what He has said in
His written Word about that area. If I have faith for protection,
He can get through to me and communicate with me about it. If I
don't, I'm likely to miss what He has to say.

The second element is prayer. Not just the telling-God-what-
I-need kind of prayer but the two-way kind of prayer that gives
Him time to talk to me in return. I learned that even though God's
Spirit can lead me and speak to me anytime, anywhere, I am better
equipped to perceive those leadings if I've spent quiet times alone
with Him getting to know His voice.

The third element is obedience. If I want to benefit from God's instructions, I have to act on them—whether those instructions come through His written Word or by the personal, inward leading of His Spirit.

Once I got those three elements in place, I felt like Watson must have felt the first time he heard Alexander Graham Bell's voice crackling through their first experimental phone line. I experienced the thrill of hearing God's protective instructions coming back at me from the other end of my prayers.

The first time I recall receiving them loud and clear, I was folded up on my knees in my walk-in closet enjoying my morning devotional time just a few months after the garage door incident. I'd been thanking God for His Psalm 91 protection over me and my family when an impression arose in my heart. I got the distinct sense I should remind my sixteen-year-old son, Aaron (who had just gotten his driver's license), to buckle his seatbelt even if he was planning to drive only a short distance from home.

The alert carried with it no feeling of fear. On the contrary, the leading seemed so peaceful and natural that I wondered if I was just making it up. *Oh well, either way,* I shrugged, as I headed toward Aaron's room, *it certainly won't hurt to remind a teenage driver about the necessity of seatbelts.*

When I told Aaron what I felt the Lord had said to me, his face flushed just red enough to let me know he'd been caught. He hadn't been bothering to use his seatbelt on short trips. He assured me, however, he would start doing so right away.

Within the week, another car slammed into Aaron's just a few blocks from our house. The impact was so horrific that his car was demolished. Or so they tell me. I never saw it again because the wrecker hauled it straight to the junkyard.

Of course, to Aaron, seeing his spiffy red-and-white independence-mobile smashed beyond recognition was a tragedy. To me, it was a triumph because he came through the wreck—with the help of his buckled seatbelt—with little more than a scratch.

Some people might say that was a coincidence. I didn't think so. I decided if I ever sensed a prompting like that in prayer again, I'd take it seriously.

That decision served me well a few years later when, once again during my morning prayer time, I noticed something was bothering me. Unlike before, however, I couldn't put my finger on what it was. I just sensed an irritation, a scratchy feeling, in my heart that I couldn't explain. Since I was in a hurry to run the errands I had planned, I tried to shrug off the feeling and get on with the business of the day.

After all, externally, everything seemed to be fine. It was a gorgeous day. My seventeen-year-old daughter, Jennifer, had headed out the door for school right on time. We hadn't even gotten into a tussle over anything before she left. Yes, it was a good day!

Yet as I scooped my car keys off the dresser and headed for the door, I couldn't escape the nagging sense that danger was lurking.

What could be wrong on a day like this? I thought. I figured I was just hormonal and jumped in the car to head across town. Still, I couldn't shake the jumpy sense that something was about to go wrong.

Praying as I drove, I asked the Lord to help me understand what He was saying to my heart. *Is there something I need to know, Father? Is trouble coming?* I pressed the accelerator as the traffic light turned green.

The air reverberated with the screech of tires and horns honking. I stomped the brakes and stopped just short of the speedster who ignored the red light and roared through the intersection, clearing my car with inches to spare. The shock set my hands to trembling on the wheel. "Thank You, Lord!" I breathed.

The near miss behind me, I realized that's what I'd been sensing. A possible wreck. Now that it was over and all was well, I could relax and enjoy my day.

Instead of relaxing, as I drove, the tension increased. Misery set in. I jumped at the rumble of an engine revving behind me. I flinched at the slightest squeak of tires on pavement. Glaring at passing motorists as if they were all out to get me, I couldn't escape the feeling that another wreck was about to happen.

That's stupid, I thought. *I'm just shaken up from the close call I had earlier. What are the odds of the devil planning two wrecks for one day? I just need to calm down.*

But, try as I might, I couldn't squelch the alarm sounding in my spirit. Instead of finishing my errands, I drove to the church and spent some time praying in the prayer room.

When I left, I felt better, but some concern still shadowed me. Back at home, I prayed a while more as the Holy Spirit led. Then I called a praying friend and told her about the situation. "Am I losing my mind?" I asked her. "I've been agitated about a wreck all day long. I've prayed about it, but I'm not quite at peace yet."

Almost before the words were out of my mouth, a sense of joy bubbled up from my heart. "Never mind!" I said. "Whatever was bothering me just vanished. It lifted like a bird taking flight. I guess everything is okay now."

I hung up the phone feeling embarrassed and, for some reason, looked at my watch. It was six o'clock. I wondered why Jennifer wasn't home yet.

A half hour later as I dragged leftovers from the refrigerator and wrapped them in foil packages to reheat them in the oven, the phone rang.

"Mom? It's Jen. I've just had a car wreck. I'm so sorry, Mom. I was driving my friend's car, and somehow I lost control...."

Her voice trembling, Jennifer described how the car had skidded across all four lanes of one of the busiest roads in town during rush-hour traffic. How it failed to collide with another car, the policeman at the scene couldn't explain. Somehow, the runaway auto had threaded its way through a maze of other vehicles without hitting any of them. It did, however, make major contact with a pole of some sort before it rolled into the roadside ditch.

The wreck took place just a couple of minutes before 6:00 p.m.

The car was full of teenagers. Not one was injured.

The insurance company paid for the damage to the car.

Man, I'm glad my spiritual cell phone didn't drop that call.

The Most Peculiar Summer of My Life

I'll be honest. For the first few years, I assumed God offered His protection to His children just for our own personal benefit. As I matured in my relationship with the Lord, however, I began to understand that, as believers, we are blessed to be a blessing. God never intended us to gather His promises around us like a fort and hide inside them, happy and safe, while the world outside goes to hell in a hand basket.

God wants us to use our connection with Him to reach out and help others who don't know how to obtain that divine help for themselves. He intends us to be conduits of His protective power—not only for fellow Christians who don't yet know how to live in His protection, but also for unbelievers.

God loves both saints and sinners. He desires to *"have mercy on all"* (Romans 11:32).

It was His intense desire to show mercy and extend His protection to all that threw me—and, no doubt, countless other praying believers—into the most peculiar season of my spiritual life. All through the summer of 2001, I was seized at intervals by an unexplainable pain—not in my body, but in my spirit. The inward agony struck at odd times and for no apparent reason. The ferocity of it often left me doubled over, weeping and praying in the spirit.

Thank God, my husband, Kelly, is a praying man and a minister well versed in the operations of the Holy Spirit; otherwise, he might have wondered if my sanity had flown the coop. He too had experienced what we sometimes call "prayer burdens," and he recognized I was carrying one. Even so, the length and fervor of this particular season of prayer seemed extreme.

One Sunday in late August as we drove home from church, he looked over at me and noticed the familiar, troubled look gathering once again on my face. "Are you okay?" he asked, his eyebrows pinched together in concern.

I felt bad for him. This odd and excruciating need to pray had interrupted our lives so many times that summer. No doubt, he was wondering if his wife would ever be normal and consistently happy again. I wanted to tell him I was fine, but I couldn't. It would have been a lie.

I leaned my head against the car window and closed my eyes to block out the dancing green foliage of upstate New York that framed the winding road to our home. I couldn't bear to look at the majestic, peaceful evergreen forest that slipped past as we drove. I didn't have the heart or the energy to peer into the sun-dappled hiding places and watch for the deer I sometimes spotted sleeping there. It annoyed rather than delighted me that hummingbirds were out there flitting and sipping from fragrant honeysuckle blossoms while ladybugs ambled up tree trunks and, when they felt like it, lifted their red and black wings for a short flight in the sunshine.

A rough spot on the asphalt jarred the car and rattled my head against the window. How was it possible for the world to seem so right and peaceful around me, when within me it seemed to writhe with violence and pain?

Poor Kelly. He'd put up with these bouts of grief-stricken prayer almost since the day we'd moved to New York three months earlier. And the awful part was, I couldn't explain them. I didn't know what I was praying about. All I knew was that when I yielded to the Holy Spirit in times of prayer, I found myself asking for mercy for souls. I felt my heart wrapping itself around the east coast of New York as if trying to hug the people there and keep them safe.

I told Kelly about it, but it all seemed so vague. So nonsensical.

"I'm sorry, honey," I said. "Maybe I can pray for a while when we get home and the pain will lift in time for us to have lunch together."

"Do whatever you need to do," he answered, his voice filled with kindness. "I understand."

A few weeks later, on the Friday night before September 11, I walked into our weekend church service carrying the same sense of pain and agitation I'd experienced off and on over the past few months. But on that night, it reached a fever pitch. As the instruments boomed praise tunes and the worship team rejoiced, I tried to shove the agony aside. I wanted to be happy and worship the Lord like normal. I wanted to raise my hands and smile and enjoy my salvation.

But the Holy Spirit wouldn't let me. There were lives on the line, and time was running out.

For the first time since the pain began, the full intensity of the tragedy that was about to strike washed over me. I couldn't sing. I couldn't smile. I couldn't rejoice. All I could do was cry.

I grabbed Kelly's arm to get his attention. "I have to leave," I whispered. "Something terrible is about to happen, and I have to pray now."

What? His eyes asked the question.

"I don't know."

Hurrying down the hallway of the church, I opened doors, searching for an empty room where I could pray alone and unheard. I could tell from the urgency in my spirit that this would not be a quiet little talk with Jesus. This was going to be the kind of authoritative, devil-resisting, top-of-my-lungs kind of prayer that would rock the walls.

I found an empty room with a solid door and shoved it closed behind me.

What happened next still amazes me and leaves me in awe of the loving, merciful God we serve. The holy wind of the Spirit blew through me and prayed the prayers only He knew to pray. Amid shouts and cries, I heard myself calling people's names one after the other, asking God to save them and protect them. I heard myself praying about the fire and the walls falling and the escapes. I wept and prayed for the protection of people I didn't know.

Some of what I was praying made sense. Some of it didn't.

What perplexed me most was why I kept praying, "Seven, seven, seven."

777.

What could the number 777 have to do with saving lives?

I don't know how long I prayed that way. All I know is that after a while, the tumult in my spirit ceased, and all was still inside me. The pain was gone. The grief had vanished. I felt normal again.

I had done my part in prayer. I'm sure that thousands of others did their part too. Only eternity will tell how many more lives would have been lost on September 11, 2001, if God's people hadn't prayed.

Perhaps eternity will also reveal that there were some who died because when God dialed the intercessors, some of the calls got dropped.

There's no need for me to rehearse what happened the day the towers fell. We all know. When I turned on the television that morning, the images explained to me in an instant the reasons behind my summer of spiritual pain. I saw firsthand what the Spirit of the Lord had been working to protect people from.

At the time, the revelation was no comfort. All I could do was weep with millions of other Americans over the lives that were lost. All I could do was reel over the realization that our world just gotten more dangerous than ever.

A few minutes later, news broke about the plane that hit the Pentagon. When I heard that it struck a section of the building that was under construction, thereby sparing many lives that otherwise would have been lost, I knew it was no coincidence. For me, the flight number told the story.

American Airlines Flight 777.

The Final Word

When the subject of God's protection comes up, people always have questions. They want to know why this person was saved from calamity and another person wasn't. They want to know why,

Part Two

ADVENTURES IN THE SHADOW OF THE ALMIGHTY

By Melanie

Part Two

ADVENTURES IN THE SHADOW OF THE ALMIGHTY

A Refuge in the Red Zone

The yellow and white tent perched amid rolling green hills outside Mozyr, Belarus, looked like a giant daffodil soaking up the last rays of sun. Long lines snaked up the hill and into the distance as three thousand people streamed into the tent.

Preparing for the service, Kevin McNulty gazed at the crowd. He and his wife, Leslie, along with their ministry team, had been at this location for almost three weeks. Although this was their first time to minister in this region of Belarus, they'd preached all over the former Soviet Union and other parts of the world. But they'd never seen a sicker group of people than these. Many suffered from angry red rashes. Some—even young people—had lost patches of hair. Others had huge chunks of flesh missing, as though eaten away by some unseen enemy. Yet God had healed so many that the crowd swelled with each service.

They couldn't have asked for a better experience, except for one thing. Members of their team were experiencing strange symptoms. Kevin looked at Leslie, who'd felt weak and tired before their arrival and now stood in faith against sickness. Several of the missionaries suffered aggravated illnesses, while an angry rash appeared on the neck of one of the team. Using all of his willpower, Kevin refused to claw at the fiery rash that had crept up his back.

Stifling a sigh, Kevin stood up to preach. The response made all their physical woes insignificant. Hundreds of people gave their hearts and lives to Jesus. "How many of you would like to be baptized?" he asked.

The crowd waved their hands in a glorious response.

"How many would like to go to the river and be baptized today?"

A hush fell over the tent as every hand fell. In silence, the crowd slipped out of the tent and went home.

What just happened? Kevin wondered, looking at Leslie with a raised brow. She shrugged. Things had been going so well.

The Red Zone

After the service, Kevin and Leslie spoke to a local pastor. "You don't understand why no one would be baptized in the river?" he said.

"No, we don't," Kevin said.

"It's because this is a radiation zone."

Kevil and Leslie stared at him in stunned silence. They knew the world's worst radiation accident had happened in Belarus at Chernobyl in 1986. They understood there was a lot of radiation in the former Soviet Union. But they were unfamiliar with the specifics. "Our ministry headquarters are in Florida, and we live in Moscow," Leslie explained. "We had no idea…"

"…that this area where you're ministering is the Red Zone," the pastor said, finishing her sentence.

"What's the Red Zone?" Kevin asked.

The pastor opened a map that showed the area in different colors. "Here's where we are," he said, pointing to a portion marked in red. "And here's Chernobyl," he said, pointing to a place a short distance away. "The Red Zone marks the hottest radiation. The government doesn't even allow Geiger counters here."

Kevin and Leslie looked at one another in shock. They'd planted their tent in the epicenter of the worst radiation in Belarus. The accident at Chernobyl, they learned, had affected a large portion of the country. Some villages had been evacuated and abandoned, but many people had returned because they had nowhere else to go.

"The rashes…" Kevin began.

"Hair loss and missing flesh…" Leslie concluded.

For almost three weeks they'd been ministering in the most dangerous levels of radiation on earth. Now everyone on the team—including them—suffered from radiation poisoning.

And they had five days left to go.

Leaving was out of the question. They may not have known that they'd pitched their tent in the Red Zone, but God knew. No wonder the crowds kept swelling. The highest percentage of kidney and liver failure was among children under the age of ten.

All forms of cancer affected the young children. These people were dying a slow and lingering death, and there was no government on earth that could help them.

Their only hope was in God, but He had to work through Kevin, Leslie, and the rest of the team. If only they didn't feel so sick. For them to continue ministering in the Red Zone, they had to find the faith not only for the sick and maimed that flocked to each service, but they also had to find faith for themselves.

Unseen Enemy

This wasn't the first time the McNultys had found themselves in a dangerous situation. A few months after they were married, they'd smuggled Bibles into China. In Beijing, they'd passed out tracks at Tiananmen Square in the days leading up to the government massacre of unarmed civilians. They'd escaped Beijing on the last train out before the rest of the trains were burned.

Although that situation had also been fraught with danger, this one was different. Police, armed soldiers, and tanks were...visible. Radiation was an unseen enemy that no border patrol could stop. It was as insidious as it was deadly. Even if they'd had access to them, there were no weapons on earth to fight radiation poisoning.

Except the Word of God.

"Either the Bible is true or it's not," Kevin said to Leslie. "We know it's true so we stake our lives on it."

Opening their Bibles to Psalm 91, they prayed it aloud together. Voices shaking with emotion, they read verse 10. *"No evil will befall you, nor will any plague come near your tent"* (NASB).

Thank God, they might have symptoms of radiation poisoning, but they had His promise in writing that no plague would come near their tent. In addition, the Lord gave Leslie Exodus 23:25. Together they prayed the Scripture over their situation. *"But you shall serve the LORD your God, and He will bless your bread and water; and I will remove sickness from your midst"* (NASB).

No plague would come near their tent, and God promised to remove sickness from their midst. It didn't get much better than that. Trusting the Lord to fulfill His promises, they continued to minister to thousands of people desperate for a touch from God.

Rebel Bombs

Three days later, they got a call from one of their ministry team in Moscow. "Another bomb has gone off in the metro," she said. "They're getting very close to your apartment."

Since Kevin and Leslie had moved to Moscow in 1993, Russia had been in an ongoing war with Chechnya. One of the bombs had exploded where their team traveled daily, and Chechen rebels threatened more. Moscow was on high alert.

We might as well face it, Kevin thought. *We're powerless against the rebel bombs.* Their only hope was in God. Kevin and Leslie had learned what so many people didn't understand. To access the promises of God and activate them, you had to take the matter up legally. You had to go to the Bible and find a promise that would back you up in heaven. Going before the Highest Court of the Universe, you had to present your case and show legal cause for God to answer your prayer. Then you had to stand on your legal right to claim that promise in front of God, the holy angels, and Satan with his crowd. Once you made your stand, you couldn't flinch or back down. Your words and your actions had to prove that you believed God's Word in spite of the circumstances.

Calling the team together, Kevin and Leslie explained the situation. "God has saved us many times when we stood on the ninety-first psalm," Leslie said. "So we're going to pray it now over the situation in Moscow and ask God to expose the bombs before they're detonated." Using Psalm 91 as their legal right to intervention from heaven, they took the matter before the High Court.

And Then There Were Three

Later that same day, Leslie got a call from one of the staff at their ministry office in Daytona Beach, Florida. "I want you to know that I'm not afraid," Joan began. "But the largest hurricane in history is heading straight for Daytona Beach. The city is being evacuated, and we have to leave."

Leslie felt like Job. One messenger after another brought grim news. Radiation poisoning. A bomb in Moscow. A hurricane in Daytona Beach. They were being hit, *hard*, at every place they had a presence. They stood to lose everything—even their lives.

Kevin and Leslie couldn't head off a hurricane any more than they could stop a bomb. They had to stand on the Word, take it before Heaven's Court, and refuse to be moved by the situation.

"Listen, Joan, I know you've got to evacuate," Leslie said, "but take a minute and open your Bible. We're going to pray Psalm 91 over the office, the staff, and the city."

Half a world apart, the two women prayed together in agreement. "*He shall cover you with His feathers, and under His wings you shall take refuge; His truth shall be your shield and buckler. You shall not be afraid of the terror by night, nor of the arrow that flies by day, nor of the pestilence that walks in darkness, nor of the destruction that lays waste at noonday*" (verses 4–6).

There was nothing to do now except trust that God was at work behind the scenes, fulfilling His promises. Kevin and Leslie did not let illness, rashes, or evil reports stop them from sharing the gospel.

Heaven Intervenes

As they continued to minister in the Red Zone, the angry red rash on Kevin's back and neck stopped its insidious advance. So miniscule was the change that, at first, the lessening of the vibrant red was not noticeable to the human eye. Neither did Leslie notice the short bursts of energy that coursed through her body, nor the slow but steady recession of the symptoms that plagued her. Symptoms or no symptoms, they went about the Father's business and trusted Him to take care of the rest.

Hurricane Floyd formed as a tropical wave off the coast of Africa on September 7, 1999, and grew into the largest Atlantic hurricane of its strength ever recorded. Rated just below a category-five status, it lashed the Bahamas with winds up to 155 miles per hour and horrific waves 50 feet high. Heading toward the United States, it precipitated the largest peacetime evacuation in the history of the country, with 2.6 million people evacuating coastal areas in Florida, Georgia, and the Carolinas.

Floyd followed every trajectory anticipated by the National Weather Service. Daytona Beach, Florida, was in his direct path. Yet without warning, on the morning of September 16, 1999, the storm did something that no computer or forecaster had predicted. Hurricane Floyd made a sharp right turn, missing Daytona Beach. In another surprise move, it diminished to a category two hurricane by the time it hit North Carolina. Even so, its winds downed hundreds of trees and damaged 357 houses. Damage to northeast Florida amounted to $46.5 million, a fraction of what had been expected.

Although Hurricane Floyd missed Daytona Beach, not long afterward the area was hit by a tropical storm. Angels were still on assignment, because when vicious winds lifted the roof off the building housing the McNultys' ministry office, the part of the roof over their offices did not budge.

The enemy continued to plot and plan destruction over the McNultys' ministry, but according to the promise in Isaiah 54, no weapon formed against them could prosper.

In Moscow, the sun had not tipped its face over the horizon when a Russian SWAT team, operating on a tip, gathered in silence outside an apartment in a high-rise building. Using an element of surprise, they stormed the apartment at 5:30 in the morning. Inside, they found a bomb set to detonate in four hours.

The apartment was just across the canal from Kevin and Leslie McNulty's home.

As a team of specialists worked to defuse the bomb, Russian police scouring the area found a Chechen storehouse just below the bus stop near the McNultys' apartment. Under the sidewalk, the rebels had stashed an entire armory of machine guns, hand grenades, bombs, bullets, and dynamite.

God had not only kept their home and ministry safe, He'd healed their bodies. Every symptom of radiation poisoning fled Kevin and Leslie's bodies and the bodies of their team members. In addition, hundreds of people in the Red Zone had been healed. On the last night of their stay in Belarus, Kevin and Leslie McNulty sang and rejoiced before God.

His Word was true; His promises were sure.

Just as Psalm 91 promised, no evil befell them.

No plague came near their tent.

The Angel of Death Passed Over

Towering pines and aspens stood like sentinels along the swollen, rushing river that swept melted snow from the Colorado mountains to the valley below. Fish darted through the crystal water, shooting above the surface in shining silver arcs before vanishing again in the swirling tide. Six-year-old Cordell Sheffield's blue eyes shone bright, his blond hair glinting in the warm sun, as he stepped onto a mossy rock to pose for a picture.

His mother, Debra, drank in the crisp air, thankful that they'd had time for this vacation with him. Cordell was the youngest of three children, his siblings much older; he'd been a surprise blessing from God.

"Okay...smile!" Cordell's father, Barry, said as he snapped a picture. "I'm going to the van to get more film, so be still."

As her husband walked away, Debra smiled at her son. He was lit up like a sparkler on the Fourth of July. Behind him, the water roared like a racecar; whitecaps slapped the rocks in their path and bounced up hard with fingers of frigid water spraying both mother and son. Cordell threw back his head and laughed with glee when they showered him, raising goose bumps on his flesh.

Somewhere amid the laughter, an angry wet surge reached up and slammed him like a fist. The force of it knocked Cordell off balance, and before Debra could reach for him, he was swept away—a twig of a boy tumbling along in the current, disappearing and bobbing up again in the froth.

"*Barry!*" Debra screamed.

Grabbing a rock in the river, Cordell held on with all his six-year-old strength. Then he felt the rock moving, giving way, and coming loose from its roots like a loose tooth when he bit into a hard apple.

The freezing water swept him farther from his family until he grabbed another rock. Holding tight, Cordell fought for his life as the water beat him without mercy and pried at his grip. He won the battle. His shivering arms strained against his foe, but the rock betrayed him. Shoved loose by the current, it sent him soaring downstream.

No! Unable to say the word with the water pounding in his face, Cordell acted it out. Resisting the pull of the river with all his might, he grabbed another rock. The water coursed above his chin but he held on anyway, tipping his head back so he could breathe.

Beneath his rigid grip, the rock trembled. It was moving... coming loose from its place.

Just as it gave way, Cordell felt another force engulf him. Strong arms gripped his flailing frame and pulled him toward the riverbank. His eardrums still battered by the sound of rushing death, Cordell found himself wrapped in his father's embrace. His dad, a Sergeant First Class in the US Army, was a strong swimmer and had managed to rescue him. His mother wrapped him in a towel, rubbing warmth back into his shivering body.

It wasn't until they had driven down the mountain that Debra's heartbeat slowed to a gallop. Dry and warm, she shivered; that had been close. None of her other kids ever had such a hair-raising brush with death. Thank God she'd always prayed that her children would live out the length of their days and they would not be cut short.

Maybe Cordell needs more prayer than the others.

Crushing News

Months later, Debra flew home from a mission trip to South Africa. Cordell bounded into her arms with the rambunctious affection of a puppy. Hugging him tight and peppering his face with kisses, Debra sighed with contentment. It was good to be home.

"While you unpack, I'm going outside to move the cars around," Barry said.

Debra looked at the stack of laundry begging to be washed. "Okay. Would you take Cordell with you?"

Cordell trotted outside after his father. He loved helping his dad. Jumping into the passenger seat of the van, he rode beside his father and watched with fascination as Barry pushed a broken Volkswagen into position for repairs and secured it with bricks under each tire. Afterwards, Barry told him to go inside; they were done for the night. Speed-walking down the hill, he heard an odd sound, like the groaning and scraping of metal. Then he heard wheels spinning. Glancing over his shoulder, he saw the Volkswagen barreling down the hill after him. Turning around to see what was happening, Cordell tripped and fell on his back.

He didn't have time to scream before the front tire, followed by the back tire, rolled over his neck, across his chest, and down his abdomen.

Tire Tracks

After unpacking and starting laundry, Debra dropped with exhaustion to the sofa. Outside, dusk had settled in; nighttime seemed to come early in rural Oklahoma. Pulling her Bible onto her lap, she opened it and started to read.

"*Go outside! Now!*" The command came from within. Before she could react, she heard another voice scream her name.

"*Debbie!*" The sound of Barry's voice propelled her out the door in a dead run.

"The car popped out of gear and ran over him!" Barry screamed. "I don't know where he is!"

Debra ran into the dark field and screamed, *"Satan, you can't have him! Father, show me where he is!"*

Without thought or premeditation she bolted across the tall grass to where Cordell lay. Alive. Using his survival training and medical knowledge, Barry checked his son with great care. "Nothing seems to be broken," he said before carrying him into the house. Tire tracks ran across Cordell's neck and chest. A deep red mark marred his abdomen. His back bled from burrs and stickers embedded there.

He had no other injury. That night, Debra stood beside Cordell's bed and watched him sleep, the moonlight casting a soft glow in his room. *That's twice*, she thought. *Whatever I prayed for the other kids isn't enough for this one. Maybe he's just accident-prone; it doesn't matter. I've got to learn more about praying protection.*

Debra dove into the Bible with the ferocity of a lioness protecting her cub. She listened to teaching tapes and gleaned insights from other more seasoned intercessors. In the process, she learned the power of praying God's Word. She grasped with thrilling clarity the reality of Hebrews 4:12: *"For the word of God is living and powerful, and sharper than any two-edged sword, piercing even to the division of soul and spirit, and of joints and marrow, and is a discerner of the thoughts and intents of the heart."*

The Blood

Once she realized how powerful Word-based prayers could be, Debra searched the Scriptures for promises of protection. She discovered Psalm 91 and began praying it over Cordell, as well as the rest of the family.

She also learned about the protective power that resides in the blood of Jesus. Studying the account in Exodus of how Moses led the Israelites out of Egyptian captivity, she was captivated by the instructions God gave to protect them from the angel of death. He told them to sacrifice a lamb without spot or blemish and to paint their doorposts with the blood. When the death angel passed over, every person and every animal belonging to those who had lamb's blood on the doorpost was protected and lived. In the Egyptian homes where the blood had not been applied, the firstborn of every family and every flock died.

Debra knew the blood of the lamb on the doorpost was symbolic of the blood of the Lamb of God—Jesus—who would one day be slain for the sins of the world. If lamb's blood under the old covenant could protect both people and animals from death, how much more the blood of Jesus!

Using her faith to apply it, Debra began praying the protective power of Jesus' blood over Cordell and the rest of her family every day.

Over the next few years, Debra had plenty of battles to face. Trouble came at her from every direction, but the near-fatal disasters in Cordell's life stopped. Debra was grateful for the reprieve. Still, she knew better than to relax her prayer vigil over her son.

Serpents and Scorpions

The Oklahoma sunshine melted over the countryside like butter over fresh-baked bread. A breeze blew the swaying green grass in waves of friendly greeting to passersby. Nine-year-old Cordell took a bucket and ambled outside to feed the chickens. When he finished, he shut the door to the hen house, but the latch didn't catch. Quicker than he could swat a fly, twenty-seven loose chickens squawked and flapped in the yard.

Trying to shoo them back into the coop, Cordell caught the attention of Crazy Gray—a Brahma cow who had earned her name. The cow was flat-out loony and mean as a rattlesnake. Riled for no good reason, except the chickens squawking, she charged Cordell. Cordell sprinted for his life, but instead of out-running her, he fell into the water tank and came up soaking wet, his blond hair plastered to his head and his jeans so heavy with water they slid low on his hips and threatened to collapse around his ankles.

"Mom!" Cordell called. "Can you help?"

Debra assessed the situation, and her lips twitched as she fought laughter, but one look at Cordell's face made her stifle it. He was sopping wet, tired, frustrated, and embarrassed. There would be plenty of time to chuckle about it later. Together they got Crazy Gray into another pasture.

Working up a sweat, Cordell chased the chickens toward Debra, using the rake to herd them toward the coop. They rounded up the birds with success until one of them scurried for cover under an old Monte Carlo—a restoration project that had never gotten off the ground.

Debra stood on one side of the car, closest to the chicken coop, and Cordell on the other. Using a rake, Cordell tried to shove the chicken out from under the car.

"*Snake.*" Cordell heard the word echo inside of him like an announcement on a loud speaker. *Probably my imagination*, he thought.

"Ouch!" Cordell said, letting out a yelp and grabbing his leg just above the knee.

"Ouch!" Cordell yelped again, falling backwards onto the hot wire fence. Draped in wet clothes, he couldn't get off before the electrical current burned through him like lightning.

"Something bit me!" he said.

Debra looked at his leg, but didn't see any mark, bite, or sting. "Come on, let's get the rest of those chickens," she said.

They worked for another thirty minutes before Cordell stopped and said, "Mom, my leg is really burning."

"Put on a pair of shorts so I can get a better look," she said.

Cordell went inside and changed clothes. Debra still didn't see anything on his leg, but chills ran up her spine when he spoke again.

"Mom, it feels numb now."

Date with Death

Debra phoned 9-1-1 and learned that an ambulance returning from another call was only a mile away. It arrived within minutes, and one of the paramedics took a look at Cordell's leg.

"Oh, yeah," he said with a sigh. "Two snake bites...here and here."

Debra grabbed her Bible and cell phone before the ambulance sped away. One of the paramedics called the nearest hospital. "We've got a snakebit kid. Do you have any antivenom for children?"

"No, sorry, we only have adult antivenom."

They called the next closest hospital...and the next. They called hospital after hospital and found the antivenom they needed was only available at Children's Hospital in Oklahoma City. They had a long drive ahead.

"I'm feeling kinda dizzy," Cordell said, his face awash in a cold sweat.

The paramedic pricked Cordell with needles. "Your son is numb to his waist," he said in a soft voice to Debra. "I don't know if he's going to make it to Oklahoma City."

Counterattack

Fear reared up and gripped Debra so hard she struggled to catch her breath. Hands shaking, she called her friends and church members for prayer. "Cordell's been double snakebit!" she said. "He needs prayer!"

As she snapped her cell phone shut, her rising panic was arrested by the husky voice of the paramedic, calm as a lake on a lazy day. "You have the answer in your lap," he said. "Why don't you open it?"

Still shaking, Debra looked down and saw what he meant—her Bible. Her phone rang, and one of her friends said, "The Lord gave me Acts 28:3 and 5 where Paul was bitten by a snake. According to the Bible he shook it off and never got sick. The Lord told me that the same thing will happen to Cordell."

Debra opened her Bible to Psalm 91 and began reading it as a prayer over her son. When she reached verse 13, she almost shouted with joy. *"You shall tread upon the lion and the* **cobra,** *the young lion and the* **serpent** *you shall trample underfoot."*

All those months she'd been praying protection for Cordell from cobras and snakes! Faith welled up in her like water in the gully after a heavy rain. Fear fled, and she took authority over the snakebite.

"In the name of Jesus, Cordell is protected from cobras, serpents, and snakes! No weapon formed against Cordell will prosper, and that includes snakebites! Cordell will live and not die! I command his body to be healed! He is under the protection of the Most High, and he's covered by the blood of Jesus!"

An hour and a half after the first snakebite, the ambulance screamed its way into Children's Hospital. After examining Cordell, the head of the children's department pulled Debra aside. "All I can say is that your son is a very lucky boy. It must have been a dry strike."

"What's that?" Debra asked.

"It means that the snake must have bitten something else before it bit Cordell."

"Ahhh…the chicken that never came out from under the car," Debra said.

"Still," said the doctor shaking his head, "a lot of people die from a dry strike. You get some venom, just not as much. There was never even any swelling, and by the time he arrived here the numbness was gone. That's pretty amazing. You can take him home."

Today, Cordell Sheffield is twelve years old, happy, healthy, and still living under the protection of the blood of Jesus.

The angel of death passed over.

❧

Hidden in the Mighty Hand of God

Irene Gleeson raised a hand to shield her eyes from the blazing red African sun. Around her, hundreds of spent bullet cartridges littered the parched earth as a stark reminder of the terror that stalked North Uganda. Mud huts dotted the horizon like clouds of dust. Digging the toe of her shoe into the cracked earth, Irene sighed under the crushing weight of the crisis that confronted her.

What on earth she was doing in this place? she wondered. Why did she ever leave the safety of her home in Australia? What had convinced her and her husband they could ever make any difference in a county so racked with horror and hatred?

Irene knew the answer even before she asked the questions.

God had called them to Uganda. That's why they had come.

But even so, they'd been unprepared for the violence of this nation—violence that had erupted under Idi Amin's reign of terror and grown worse as rebel troops raped, tortured, and murdered innocent people. In recent years, thousands of children had been kidnapped and sold into the Sudan slave trade. Countless others had been trained as soldiers to perpetuate the atrocities. Now almost two million people—all of them too terrified to stay in their homes, many of them ravaged by HIV/AIDS—were starving to death in camps.

Walking back to the orphanage she'd started under a mango tree near the Sudan border, Irene looked across the sea of ebony faces. No child's eyes should be shuttered with the kind of agony she saw reflected in theirs.

Lord, she was their only hope. A chill rippled across her scalp at the thought. Helping orphans of war had seemed a lofty goal back home when she was surrounded by her children and grandchildren. It hadn't dawned on her then that, in Uganda, there were no red crosses or white flags that marked good Samaritans off-limits to the terrors of war. She and her husband had been naïve about what they were going to face. They had no idea they would live every day perched on the edge of eternity, staring death in the eye.

Irene's husband had quickly crumbled under the pressure. He left her alone while he sought to regain his stability in a distant city, then decided he wanted out of both Uganda and his marriage. He had mailed Irene the divorce papers with a simple message, "Sorry, I'm not coming back."

Now, she faced her future as a retired school teacher…a white woman…a grandmother…alone…in the middle of a war zone marked by terrorists. But that wasn't even the worst of it. The most frightening thing was the revelation that had settled over her like the sweltering heat: *Her love for God wasn't enough to keep her alive in this place. She needed supernatural protection, and she wasn't sure how to get it.*

God did have power enough to protect her. Irene was sure of that. It was one reason she had become a Christian. Before she was born again, she'd gotten her fill of powerless gods as a practicing Buddhist. Visiting the shrine room of a Buddhist monastery, she'd been shocked to see that someone had knocked Buddha's head off. It lay broken and forgotten on the floor where it fell.

"Why don't you fix it?" she'd asked.

"Let it be," she'd been told.

Buddha has no power! How useless is that?

Now she looked at the throng of Ugandan children, filthy with neglect, their heads caked with dust and sores, their skin lumpy with scabies. Their sticky faces were covered with flies, their eyes haunted, and their bellies empty.

If there is power and protection in Jesus, then, Lord, You've got to teach me how to access it. Otherwise we'll all die.

Beloved of God

Depressed over her husband's defection, and feeling fright-ened, rejected, and alone, Irene found comfort in the Song of Solomon. The tenderness of it ministered healing to her wounded heart. She especially loved the phrase "My beloved is mine, and I am his!" (See Song of Solomon 6:3.)

One night after staring into the darkness, rehearsing those words in her mind, Irene climbed out of bed and lit a candle. Using fluorescent chalk, she wrote them on the ceiling. Each time she woke—alone—she gazed at the words.

Irene was still naïve about war some nights later when torch-lights flickered outside her window in the darkness. Opening the door, she stepped out to see who was there. "What do you want?" she asked in a civilized manner.

She expected a civilized answer, but she never received it.

Instead, she staggered back in terrified shock as five men lunged at her from the shadows, shoving guns and bayonets toward her chest. *I'm going to die*, she realized, squeezing her eyes closed against the chilling sneer on her killer's face. *The next person I see will be Jesus.* She heard the rebels loading their guns and braced for the worst.

Nothing.

Opening her eyes again, Irene watched in wonder as the rebels stabbed at her with bayonets and guns. In a kind of bizarre ballet, they danced about, thrusting and parrying with murderous intent—unable to kill her. She seemed to be protected behind an invisible shield.

"*The name!*" The Holy Spirit's instruction came to her with authority.

She pointed to the rebels and shouted, "In the name of Jesus—you *go!*"

They fled. Shivering under the covers on her bed, she heard gunfire in the distance. Others, she knew, had not found the protection she did. *So…there's great power in the name of Jesus.* She sat awake the rest of the night pondering that power.

It Shall Not Come Near You

Searching the Bible, Irene was astounded to find many promises of protection in it. The most wonderful were in Psalm 91. They seemed almost too good to be true. *"A thousand may fall at your side, and ten thousand at your right hand; but it shall not come near you"* (verse 7). That was some promise. Was it possible to live in the middle of this insanity and survive? Could those words, written by David thousands of years ago, really protect a frightened grandmother in war-torn Uganda today?

Convinced the answer was yes, Irene began praying Psalm 91 over her orphans, her staff, and herself. She ordered a ministry tape of the psalm and played it for the children. Daily, she taught them to pray. Daily, she taught them what she'd learned about divine protection. With God's help, they made it through the year alive.

Another New Year's Eve marked a change in the calendar, but it did not mark a change in the rape, torture, and murder that had brought a people to its knees in terror. Instead, the rebels' rampages forced the whole area into a blackout. There could be no light, not a single flicker to draw the terrorists' attention. Shivering in the dark, Irene could feel death in the air. One thought hammered at her mind.

The rebels are going to kill us all!

During the cold, bleak night, Irene's radio station played a recording of Psalm 91.

> *You shall not be afraid of the terror by night, nor of the arrow that flies by day, nor of the pestilence that walks in darkness, nor of the destruction that lays waste at noonday. A thousand may fall at your side, and ten thousand at your right hand; but it shall not come near you.* (verses 5–7)

Morning dawned bright and clear, the sun a beacon of hope as it peeked over the horizon. Thousands of children, dozens of staff…all were alive and well. The murderers, Irene learned, had passed them by, going south to pillage and plunder another area.

There's no such thing as luck in a war zone, Irene thought. *God divinely protected us. Psalm 91 is as true today as it was the day it was written.*

Message of Hope

Irene used her radio station to broadcast the gospel, blaring the good news for miles. In a land filled with hopelessness, it was the only message of hope. While most within hearing distance appreciated the message, the rebels did not. On the road one night, rebel troops pulled her over.

"Stop broadcasting that Jesus stuff over the radio or we'll blow up the radio station!" they warned.

Irene knew that "Jesus stuff" was what stood between her and her orphans and a torturous death. She would never stop broadcasting the gospel, nor would she stop praying. "Lord, Your Word says that the wicked will stand confused at the gates of the righteous. Please confuse the wicked that have set themselves against us."

Sure enough, God answered that prayer. The rebels became so confused that they blew up the wrong radio station. Irene went on broadcasting the gospel.

In November 1999, she awakened to the sound of rattling at her door. Torchlight flickered through the window at 2:30 in the morning. "Who's there?" she demanded.

"Open de door!"

Alone on school property at the time, Irene peeked through the window and gasped at what she saw: twenty men with bayonets and guns surrounded her sleeping quarters. "Open de door!" they demanded.

Refusing to yield to their demand, Irene took a deep breath and shattered the quiet night with a piercing scream. Enraged, the men smashed the windows with their rifle butts, ripped the aluminum door off its hinges, and stormed into the room. Shoving bayonets and guns in her face they shouted, "Give us de money! Where's de money?"

They pushed her backwards onto the bed where she waited, trembling, for the worst. Looking up, she saw the words written across the ceiling in fluorescent chalk. *My beloved is mine, and I am His.*

I belong to God! Courage coursed through her veins, dispersing the fear. Struggling to sit up, she acted like the beloved of God. "Don't you *dare* touch me!" she shouted. "I belong to God. If you touch me, God will *get you!*"

Backing away from her, they ransacked the cupboards, grabbing a stash of dollar bills and a video camera before disappearing into the night.

With the door missing, Irene shivered in the cold night air as she talked to God. "I feel defeated," she said. "Why did You let that happen?"

"Not a hair on your head was harmed," the Lord reminded her.

"Then give me a word to comfort me."

By candlelight she read Psalm 94:17, "*Unless the* L*ord* *had been my help, my soul would soon have settled in silence.*"

"Oh, Lord, I thank You for saving my life!" She spent the rest of the night in praise and thanksgiving to God.

Sweet Sleep

As Irene continued to search the Bible for promises of protection, she realized that the foundation of them all was her covenant with God. That's why she especially loved to read Leviticus 26. The whole chapter taught Irene the power of covenant, but the Scripture she clung to was verse 6: "*I will give peace in the land, and you shall lie down, and none will make you afraid.*"

It was difficult for Irene to imagine lying down to sleep at night and not being afraid. But she claimed the promise as her own anyway and determined to live by it. Her determination was soon put to the test.

A girl who'd been kidnapped by the rebel troops managed to escape and took refuge in Childcare Kitgum, Irene's orphanage. When the rebels found out, they vowed revenge. Breathless messengers came rushing through the bush with a warning for Irene. "The rebels are coming tonight for you and the girl you're protecting!"

Irene looked around the compound. What was she to do, hide behind a few thousand orphans? Even if she had the money, what army could she hire to protect them? She had no earthly defense against the murdering bands that had run two million terrified people out of their homes. She had nothing to protect her—except the Word of God. But Irene knew now, that Word was enough.

She had confidence in the protection of her divine covenant. She believed that angels stood guard around her and her orphans just as the Bible promised. Going about her day, she finished teaching classes and tucked the young girl who had turned to her for help into bed.

In her own quarters, Irene looked at the words on her ceiling. She belonged to God. Opening her Bible, she read Leviticus 26 by the quivering light of a candle. The words of verse 9 became her prayer. "*I will give peace in the land, and you shall lie down, and none will make you afraid,*" she said.

Believing the words were true, she closed her eyes and slept.

At midnight, she awoke to the sound of gunshots. "*You shall lie down, and none will make you afraid,*" she whispered. She declared Proverbs 14:19, "*The enemy shall stand confused at the gates of the righteous.*" Somewhere nearby, the ring of an ax destroying everything in its path echoed in the darkness.

"I will live in peace here in Kitgum," she declared. "I will lie down, and no one will make me afraid." In the sudden silence, she fell asleep.

At first light, Irene heard birds chirping. Crawling out of bed, she ventured outside. The girl under her protection was asleep, safe in her bed.

The rebels had ransacked the place across the street.

Badlands and Bandits

As the years passed, it became impossible to count the number of times the rebels failed to find Irene. Blinded and confused by

God's protective power, they couldn't even grab her when she was walking in plain sight with bags of money in her hand. Irene knew the cash made her a target for them, but she had to carry it. She had no other choice.

Because of the war, Kitgum had no bank. So when people sent funds to help support the orphanage, their contributions were deposited into a bank in a city 350 miles away. To make payroll, Irene traveled to the city and withdrew money. Carrying cash, she traveled ten hours back by bus, arrived in Kitgum around midnight, and walked two kilometers to the orphanage.

When word came from a reliable source that Irene had been targeted by the rebels who knew she carried cash, Irene continued making her bank runs as usual. With no other way to bring the money back to the orphanage, she had to trust God to protect her. The nights were still, the darkness velvet each time Irene walked the dusty road home with the money in her hand. The orphanage had no electricity, no telephone lines, and no running water. There were no streetlights to light the way.

Her only protection from bandits was the Word of God.

"*Your word is a lamp to my feet and a light to my path,*" she declared (Psalm 119:105). Years passed and her staff grew, as did the cash required to pay them. Not once did the rebels find her. God lit the path for her, but He hid her path from them.

Dispelling the Darkness

It was not until 2004, however, that Irene's orphans understood the true power of their prayers for protection. During that year, the rebels swept through the area in a massive attack and abducted one hundred children—including two girls from Childcare Kitgum. Cold, wet, and hungry, the kidnapped children were forced to march all night through swamp and bush. The next day, the rebels gathered the exhausted youngsters.

"We want those who are literate and can write letters!" they demanded.

The two girls from Irene's orphanage stepped forward. "We can write," they said.

"You're from Childcare Kitgum! You people are always praying, praying, praying. You make trouble for us. Get away from us! We don't want you here! Go away!"

Using bayonets, the men drove the children away. Alone, the girls forged their way back through swamps and bush, walking all night through land filled with ambushes and land mines to get home.

Back at the orphanage, they stood in front of the other children and told their story. "Our prayers are powerful!" they said. "We have the devil on the run!"

It's been sixteen years since Irene Gleeson left her home in Australia and founded Childcare Kitgum Servants in the most dangerous part of Uganda. Strengthened by God's Word in 1 Chronicles 28:10, Irene heard the Lord say, "I have chosen you to build a sanctuary. Be strong and do it!" In obedience, she built permanent complexes comprising registered schools, kitchens, clinics, and churches. Thousands of destitute children enrolled. Hundreds of African staff were recruited.

Irene has dug wells to bring water to the parched earth. She has built a hospice for those dying of HIV/AIDS. She not only feeds 7,500 children a day, but she and her staff provide an education that takes them from preschool all the way through vocational college. Some of the first children she rescued are now teachers, builders, welders, and mechanics. All of them are servants of the Most High God, whose prayers shake the powers of darkness.

They are born-again believers who have survived the devil's most ruthless attacks by taking refuge in the mighty hand of God.

~

HEEDING THE CALL

The night washed over Dieter Tripke like India ink. Few stars shone through the cloud cover overhead. The moon's pale face, shrouded in darkness, hovered at half-mast. Yawning as he climbed into the Kenworth Classic tow truck, Dieter noted the time: *2 a.m.* He'd been hired to tow two cars from his hometown of Kelowna, British Columbia, to Vancouver before starting the long trek home. There was no time for rest; he had a job at a pest control company the following day. After that he would find something—painting or digging a well—to pay the bills and put food on the table.

Dieter's wife, Diana, and their three children were visiting family in Prince George. He ached to be with them, but since he wasn't vacationing with them this time, he would at least make the most of the time by taking as many jobs as possible.

Exhaustion wore against him like sandpaper behind his eyelids as he pulled the tow truck onto the highway. It was tough working so many jobs while pastoring Victory Life Fellowship, but it was a small church, and Dieter did what he needed to do to supplement the income that the church was not yet able to provide. The way Dieter figured it, pastoring was a lot like marriage—you were in it for the long haul, for better or for worse.

Things were worse right now, but they'd get better.

Soon, he hoped…but in the meantime, he was willing to be patient.

Dieter had known from the start that building a Word church in Canada wouldn't be easy. Christian churches needed a lot of perseverance just to survive in the country. Many of those that dug in their heels and kept going stayed small. Like a flower taking root in hard and rocky soil, they might be stunted but were grateful to be alive.

Dieter didn't resent working so hard, nor did he resent the opposition that came his way. Years ago, he'd read a book entitled *Don't Blame God* that put such things in perspective. It helped him understand, for the first time, that God wasn't out to get him; He was out to bless Him. God is good, loving, and long-suffering, all the time.

The devil, however, was another story. He was a liar who did horrible things, then laid the blame on God. That truth had marked a turning point in Dieter's life. Once he realized that Jesus came to bring abundant life, but Satan came to kill, steal, and destroy, the bad things that sometimes happened to good people began to make sense. And when he learned that Satan's schemes could be undone by the youngest and weakest child of God who learned to hear the voice of the Holy Spirit, his fears gave way to faith.

Blinking against fatigue, Dieter gripped the wheel and kept his eyes on the asphalt ribbon that snaked its way across the country.

Behind the Veil

Rumbling down the highway, Dieter had no way of knowing that he'd struck some powerful blows to the enemy, and Satan had put a contract out on him. Granted, it was a spiritual contract, but every bit as dangerous as an assassin's bullet.

Nor did Dieter know that three weeks earlier two women in his church had picked up a warning from the Holy Spirit that they should pray for his protection from an accident.

He didn't know that three days earlier his wife had been gripped with a chilling sense of danger while taking their three children on a walk. Diana had been so alarmed by the sensation; she'd stopped and pulled the children close. Feeling a great sense of foreboding, they'd prayed for Dieter's safety and protection.

Nine hours into his journey, Dieter was aware of nothing more than the need to stay awake and focused. He slid a teaching tape into the stereo and turned up the volume.

Back home, a chill rippled down the arms of Lindsay McCallum as she prayed with her prayer group at school. *Something's wrong,* she thought as spiritual alarms rang a warning in her heart. Looking up, she said, "We need to pray for Pastor Dieter!" Taking her lead, they prayed.

11:30 a.m. Ursula Tripke, Dieter's mother, knelt in the graveyard and pulled weeds from two graves. She sighed. Even now it was hard to believe she'd outlived both of her husbands. The first headstone had the name Waldemar Tripke engraved on it. The second read Gustav Issler. Between the two was an empty plot she'd reserved for herself. Someday she would rest between the two men she'd loved. Overcome with a sense of morbidity, she could almost see her own tombstone.

What's wrong with me? she wondered. Tears coursing down her face, she looked again at her burial plot. It wasn't her name on the tombstone that kept flashing before her eyes. It was *Dieter's!*

"Lord, Dieter's in trouble! Please help me to pray!" Kneeling at the unmarked grave, she pled for her son's life.

Countdown to Eternity

Noon. Dieter had delivered the two cars and was deadheading back home. After stopping at a weigh station, he started the last leg of the journey.

Around a bend on the road ahead, a man driving a semi missed his turn. Unsure which way to go, he stopped to get his bearings. He didn't take the time to pull off the road onto the shoulder. Nor did he turn on his hazard lights. Trying to figure out which way to go, he stopped the semi in the road…and parked.

The massive tow truck barreled around a curve at 62 miles an hour. Dieter gasped when he saw an 18-wheeler parked in his lane. He had no time to slow his rig or stop. Trying to swerve, he plowed into the semi.

The force of the impact imploded the tow truck. In a cacophony of screeching tires, screaming metal, and shattering glass, the cab ripped away from the deck of the truck like a pop-top on a soda can, and the driver's door was stripped away.

Ten cars back, a paramedic jumped out of his vehicle and sprinted to the wreckage. Stunned that a tow truck could be torn apart like a tinker toy, he looked around for something to cover the body. There was no way anyone in that tow truck could have survived.

Running alongside the wreck, he stopped cold. The only thing left of the cab was the passenger door and the driver's seat.

The driver was still strapped in it.

Alive.

The Goodness of God

The paramedic blinked at Dieter. "The 'Big Guy' was taking care of you," he said. "Where do you hurt?"

"I'm not hurt," Dieter explained. "Help me down, but don't drop me. I've seen you guys in the movies, and I don't want a broken leg," Dieter said with a chuckle.

He can't be joking. He must be in shock.

"I can't let you up. You're in shock, and you probably have internal injuries."

"I'm telling you, I'm fine," Dieter insisted.

He couldn't be fine, and everyone knew it. Dieter was rushed by ambulance to Hope Hospital, where he underwent a thorough exam, X-rays, and a battery of tests. He had no head injury, no spinal injury, no whiplash, no broken bones, and no internal injuries.

All they found was a cut on his right ear.

The man driving the semi also walked away unharmed.

Three weeks later, Dieter and his son visited the salvage yard and saw what was left of the tow truck. Staring at the wreckage, Dieter knew that there was no logical reason for him to be alive.

He would be dead—his life cut short, his wife a widow, and his children fatherless—if not for the prayers and intercession from ordinary people in his church. Staring at the wreckage, Dieter knew that the members of his church had learned to hear the voice of God and heed the call to pray. He was thrilled to be alive; he was proud to be their pastor.

Turning to leave, a smile tugged at Dieter Tripke's lips and lit his eyes. Being a pastor of a church was a lot like marriage—you were in it for the long haul, for better or for worse.

It doesn't get much better than this.

⌣

Tight Places

Soft laughter rose and fell amid the sound of ice tinkling against glasses as Eloise Wright paused to look at her watch.

Midnight! The evening had begun with dinner and ended with the Silver Quill Awards. The crowd had moved from the banquet hall to the multilevel open areas where writers continued to spin their tales and swap stories. Eloise always enjoyed the district conference and usually traveled a good distance to attend. This year, however, the Dallas chapter of the International Association of Business Communicators was hosting the conference. Seeing no point in paying for a room in her hometown, Eloise had opted to drive to the North Dallas hotel each day.

Scanning the room, she realized that everyone else had only a short elevator ride before going to bed. She faced a forty-minute drive, and she'd promised to be back early to help with registration. Tearing herself away from the festivities, Eloise smoothed her burgundy suit and said goodnight.

The lobby was deserted as she crossed the lush carpet to the front door. Across the parking lot, near the freeway, her white Camry awaited her, illuminated amid the shadows by a pool of light spilling from two streetlights nearby. The car wasn't far, but even so, Eloise dreaded the walk. Her new black shoes had looked fabulous, she admitted, but after an entire evening in them, every step had become a crucible of pain.

I can't wait to get these shoes off! she thought, clicking her keyless entry to unlock her car. Sliding into the driver's seat with a sigh of relief, she reached to close the door...and looked down the barrel of a gun.

Frozen like a deer in headlights, Eloise blinked against the apparition before her. The man's face was distorted, pushed flat like a Cabbage Patch doll by the nylon hose he wore over his head. He was young, no more than a teenager. He wore sneakers, jeans, and a faded blue sweatshirt with the hood pulled up over his head. So thin he looked emaciated, he appeared to be a young man whose diet consisted of little more than drugs. She could smell his fear, but more than that she sensed a kind of ravenous hunger born of desperation that made him all the more dangerous.

Snake Eyes

"Give me your purse, or I'll blow your head off." She'd been right—he was young, but there was no mistaking the intent of his words. The gun never wavered; the black barrel looked like snake eyes beaded on her forehead. *God help me.*

Without conscious thought, Eloise pulled her makeup bag from her purse. What would he need with her makeup? she wondered with a kind of hysteria. She handed over her purse.

"I want *everything* in your purse, or I'll blow your head off!" he growled, his voice raspy through the hose. Still in stunned disbelief, Eloise handed him her makeup bag.

"Get out of the car," he ordered.

Eloise climbed out of the Camry, her feet screaming against the black pumps, her mind screaming against the gun.

"Open the trunk!" he ordered.

She complied.

"Now get inside," he growled.

"Uh...well...I don't think there's room," Eloise said, her voice as frayed as her nerves.

"Get in the trunk!" he ordered, finishing with the threat of a head shot.

Eloise closed her fist around the keys and climbed into the trunk, careful to face the backseat. The trunk closed with a *thud* followed by what sounded like the *click* of the car doors locking... or were they unlocking?

"Don't undo what's been done!" The warning dropped into her heart like a bomb exploding with implications. She held the car keys in her fist, careful not to push the buttons.

Hidden in God

Enveloped in darkness, Eloise heard the sound of her racing heartbeat thundering in her ears. The night was quiet; she couldn't tell if her abductor had run away or if he lingered, realizing that she still held the keys to the car and he couldn't steal it.

First things first. With a groan of relief, she kicked off her shoes. *Now I can think!*

She'd been careful to position herself facing the backseat because she thought it her best chance of escape. Now, on clearer consideration, it didn't seem so wise. Even if she could find a way to unlock the oval lock on the back of the seat without a light, in order to fold the seat down, a button on either side of the headrests had to be activated from *inside* the car.

"Lord," she prayed, "I don't know what's happening here, but I know I'm going to be fine. It's not time for me to die. There's too much that I haven't done yet. Even if I have to stay in this trunk all night, I know I'm going to be fine. I'm going to be at peace because I trust You to get me out of this trunk and this situation."

She tried to estimate how much time had passed since her abductor locked her in the trunk. Probably ten to fifteen minutes, long enough for him to have gotten away if he was going.

"Help!" she screamed, the word echoing back at her like a boomerang. There had been no one in the lobby or the parking lot when she left. Screaming, she realized, would exhaust her and use up the available oxygen. Feeling around in the darkness, her finger brushed the oval lock on the back of the seat.

"Push! Just push!" The command arose from her spirit with such authority that Eloise pushed the lock as hard as she could. The backseat fell forward.

Confrontation

Shocked, Eloise looked through the opening…straight into the eyes of her abductor. Standing outside the driver's door, his eyes met hers in a flash of fear and recognition. He'd removed the hose from his head; she saw his face.

At the same instant, both of them looked at the door locks. *Down!* The car was locked! He couldn't get to her without breaking a window or shooting her through the glass. Either would attract the attention of traffic from the freeway just in front of her car.

Turning, he fled behind the car, disappearing into the night.

Eloise crawled through the small opening onto the backseat. What now? Was he out there, hiding behind a nearby vehicle until she emerged? She felt like a sitting duck, shivering at the thought of the gun.

I'll drive to the hotel lobby! Crawling into the driver's seat, she hit a button on her keyless entry. The car's security system thought someone was trying to steal the car. It wouldn't start.

I've sabotaged my own car! Eloise thought with frustration.

"Lord, You got me this far. Now please help me get to the lobby!" Unlocking the door, she bolted from the car and sprinted barefoot across the parking lot to the lobby. Inside, the gathering had just broken up, and Eloise was surrounded by a security guard and friends and associates from the conference.

"All my identification with my address was in my purse," she explained to the policeman who took the report, "along with a key to my apartment." Three people from the conference drove Eloise home to get her clothes and then drove her to a friend's house. It was four o'clock in the morning when she finished canceling her credit cards.

When she finally went to bed and turned off the light, the Holy Spirit spoke to her again. *"You know I'm there for you, especially in the tight places."*

The man who abducted Eloise Wright at gunpoint was never apprehended, but she continues to live each day with the assurance that God will be with her in all of life's tight places.

And He'll be with you in yours.

⌒

EYE OF THE STORM

A balmy breeze rustled through the palm trees in Ft. Lauderdale, Florida, as twenty-five-year-old Ron Harris hurried across the airport terminal to his gate. Traffic had been gridlocked, and the line at the car rental office had crept like a lazy lizard on a hot rock. Ron glanced at his watch. If he missed Delta Flight 191, he would miss his connecting flight from Dallas to Oklahoma City, where his wife of two years, DeeAnn, awaited him.

"There's our gate!" Ron said to Bill Lackey, the businessman striding along beside him. At fifty, Bill was a big man, well over six feet tall, with sandy hair highlighted with flecks of gray. Full of energy and enthusiasm, he was one of the founders of Federal Express.

Ron, a CPA, had traveled to Ft. Lauderdale to handle a financial audit for him. Bill could have taken a more direct route home to Little Rock, but he'd opted to fly with Ron so they could work during the flight.

Relieved to be on the plane, the pair edged their way down the aisle of the Lockheed Martin L-1011 to seats 27A and 27B, located over the left wing. Ron buckled himself into the window seat while Bill settled into the seat on the aisle. Pulling out notebooks and pens, the two ordered coffee and went to work.

Time slipped by, and before they knew it, the trip was almost over. As they approached DFW airspace, however, the captain turned on the seat belt sign, asked everyone to remain seated, and explained that a fast-approaching thunderstorm with a wall cloud had complicated conditions. All planes on approach were circling as they evaluated the storm. If they couldn't land, they might fly on to Oklahoma City.

That would be great, Ron thought as he looked out the window at the driving rain and lightning. The turbulence made their work more difficult, but Ron and Bill soldiered on, making use of the time.

In the cockpit, the captain watched a Learjet maneuver out of the long line of circling planes, fly into the black cloud, and land. Following the Learjet's lead, the big Lockheed Martin whipped out of rotation and plunged into the wall cloud.

Throttle high against whipping winds, the L-1011 flew straight into the eye of the storm where the windless calm made it drop like a stone. The plane's nose dove toward the ground, then rose as the pilot backed off the throttle, losing tail speed. Moments later, it emerged from the eye of the storm only to have the wind slap it down with a vengeance.

Ron heard the landing gear grind into place beneath his seat. Bill, a pilot, looked out the window at the black cloud and knew they were too low and too slow to recover.

"Are we in trouble?" Ron asked.

"I believe so," Bill said. "Get into crash position."

Both men folded themselves down, arms locked around their knees, bracing themselves, as wild winds slammed the plane and hail mixed with rain pummeled it without pity.

What's happening? Ron lifted his head high enough to look out the window and gasped at the scene before him. Just a few feet below, he could see the wide eyes of horrified drivers in Dallas' Friday afternoon rush-hour traffic. The plane skipped across the highway, hitting cars and sheering the top off of a Mustang. Winds whipping at 90 miles per hour jerked the plane like a marionette. Streetlights flickered on early in the storm's darkness, casting an eerie glow over the scene.

"Get down!" Bill ordered, his long arm snaking out to shove Ron back into crash position. The plane pitched left, and the wing under Ron's seat hit the ground first. The scream of twisting, ripping metal raked the air as the cabin lights blinked on and off. Seconds later the plane burst into a ball of fire and slammed into the two water towers that stood on the edge of airport property. Splitting upon impact, it broke in half just behind Ron and Bill's seats.

The forward section disintegrated in the explosion.

The Call

At home, DeeAnn Harris opened the door to find her mother almost hysterical. "There's been a plane crash in Dallas," she said. "Ron's on that plane!"

"What are you talking about?" DeeAnn asked. "What makes you think Ron's on the plane that crashed?"

"I just *know* it," she insisted. "I can feel it."

DeeAnn flipped on the television. They were still watching the news when she got the call. The color drained from her face as she turned to her mother. "You were right. Ron was on that plane." Picking up the phone, she called Ron's parents.

At home in Duncan, Oklahoma, Ron's parents were stunned to hear that their son was on the plane that crashed. Even so, their response was predictable. They did the single most important thing that they'd done for their children every day of their lives: they covered him in a cocoon of prayer. Then they sent a prayer alert to their church and to friends and family across the nation. "Ron was on the plane that crashed! *Pray!*"

Field of Fire

Ron blinked as he regained consciousness. Still fastened to this seat, he was lying facedown on the runway, beaten by rain and hail. Huddling under the seat for protection, Ron realized that most of his body had been burned. His clothes had burned away, leaving him nearly naked. Looking to the right, he realized that his seat was still attached to Bill's. *Bill must be in better shape than I am,* Ron thought, noticing that Bill was almost fully clothed.

"Bill!" Ron called, nudging his shoulder. *"Bill!"*

There was no response.

Looking up, Ron took in the scene of the crash. It looked like a war zone; no…it looked like hell. Parts of the plane, bodies, baggage, and debris littered the area, all of it on fire. Orange flames licked the stormy sky like a hungry monster, greedy for more.

Looking around, he saw the tail of the plane. *Where's the front?* he wondered.

As shock wore off, the nerves in his body, exposed by burns, stood up and screamed as rain and chunks of hail pounded him. Something was wrong with his left arm. Focusing on his wounded arm, Ron blinked. Most of the forearm was missing. The outer flesh burned away, the inside of it lay exposed. The major tendons were gone. One by one, he moved the fingers on his left hand.

How is that possible?

His left leg, severed at the knee, was held together by a flimsy strip of flesh on the back side. Using his right hand, Ron wrapped his fingers around the almost amputated stump of his left leg. Issuing an order from his brain, he flexed the toes on his left foot.

How can they move? he asked himself in amazement. As he began to grasp the extent of his wounds, another question plagued Ron. Why hadn't he bled to death instantly? There was no explanation; no answer in the storm.

Vicious winds whipped his wounded body so hard that Ron closed his eyes against the pain. *I survived the crash. Now it looks like a tornado will kill me.*

The Secret Place

In the midst of it all, an incredible peace wrapped itself around Ron like a soft blanket. He *knew* that Presence. It was God. It felt as though, exposed as he was to the elements, he was in the eye of the storm, that place of perfect peace. The Bible called it the secret place of the Most High.

Wave after wave of gratitude to God washed over him. His mind flashed back to his childhood. He remembered his father, a patient man, helping him memorize Philippians 4:13, *"I can do all things through Christ who strengthens me."*

Lying in his own blood, his burns exposed to the storm, Ron spoke the words over and over. *"I can do all things through Christ who strengthens me."*

He'd known his whole life that *whatever* lay ahead, Jesus would be with him. The words of that verse had never been as poignant as they were now, facedown in the middle of a raging storm, the aircraft burning in red-hot flames of fire.

"Father, thank You for protecting me during the plane crash," Ron prayed against the driving rain. "Now Lord, I ask that You protect me from these injuries and from the storm. Keep me safe, Lord. I pray in Jesus' name."

Braving the Storm

In the distance, Ron saw a lone man bent halfway to the ground, struggling to walk against the howling gale. He waved at Ron to acknowledge that he'd seen him.

"My name is Jerry Fenske," he said, kneeling despite the savage storm. He tightened a tourniquet above Ron's left knee, then looked him in the eye. "I'm going to get help," he said.

An ambulance and fire truck arrived on the scene, but the paramedics were unwilling to brave the horrific storm. "You've got to help him now!" Jerry begged through an open window. "He's burned so bad!"

They refused to get out until the storm abated. "At least move the fire truck over to give him some protection!" Jerry demanded. As the truck idled to a stop next to Ron, he felt the heat from the engines on his burned flesh.

The peace that enveloped Ron didn't lift. When the paramedics finally loaded him into a helicopter to be flown to a large trauma center, his calm demeanor shocked them.

"My name is Ron Harris," he said. "I'd appreciate it if someone would call my wife, DeeAnn. The phone number is...."

Stunned by his lack of panic and his articulate answers, the paramedics pulled him out of the helicopter and sent him by ambulance to a small hospital in Bedford, Texas.

Sixty percent of Ron's body was burned, including his face. His ears were almost burned off. His lungs were so damaged by the fire that he was put on a ventilator to breathe.

Two days later, Ron was flown by medical flight to the burn unit at Baptist Medical Center in Oklahoma City where he underwent the first of nineteen surgeries. Of all his injuries, it was the burns to his face that DeeAnn knew would bother him most. As part of her daily prayer vigil, she asked God to heal his face without scars.

Ron Harris was one of twenty-eight people to survive the crash. The death toll was 137; among them, Bill Lackey.

It's been twenty-two years since the crash of Delta Flight 191. Although Ron walks with a limp, there isn't a single scar on his face. Not only did God heal his body, but the powerful peace that enveloped him in the middle of that inferno was a healing balm to his emotions. Today, he flies without qualm. He knows that no matter what tragedies may befall the life of a Christian, through prayer, you can ride them out in the eye of the storm.

⌒

A POWERFUL WEAPON OF WAR

Hardie Higgins stepped out of the commander's office and paused to look around the lush German countryside where he and the soldiers of the 130th Engineer Brigade had been stationed for the past few months. The place seemed peaceful, but so had America thirteen months ago. Then, without warning, that peace had been shattered by the terrorists who flew commercial airliners filled with innocent civilians into the World Trade Center and the Pentagon.

Hardie thought again—as he had so many times—about the fourth plane that missed its target that day because of the heroism of a few good people. The men and women who attacked the terrorists aboard United Airlines Flight 93 were a lot like the men and women of the 130th Brigade. They were willing to die to protect their country from terrorists.

The group on Flight 93 had finished their battle. For the soldiers of the 130th, the fight had just begun. They were about to leave Germany for the Middle East. They would go first to Kuwait, and then to Iraq.

Hardie had wanted to be in the military and to defend the United States of America—the greatest place on earth to live— since he'd been a kid. When God called him into the ministry, Hardie had run the other way; he'd volunteered for Vietnam. But even in the jungles of Southeast Asia, he couldn't escape the dealings of God. Eventually he'd gone back to college and then attended seminary.

On September 3, 1984, Hardie had been commissioned as a chaplain in the United States Army. Since then, he'd prayed for the troops, counseled them, and led worship services, making sure their religious needs were met. He went wherever they went; he ate whatever they ate; he slept wherever they slept. But there was one major difference between Hardie and the other soldiers.

He wasn't allowed to carry a weapon.

Hardie was philosophical about death. It was simple: war and death were as inseparable as life and oxygen. People were going to die in a war—there was no getting around it. Of course, the government did all they could do to minimize the number of casualties. They trained their troops well. They provided the best weapons, equipment, strategies, and surveillance available.

A Legacy Learned

In much the same way, Hardie did all he could do as a chaplain to minimize the risk to his troops—through prayer. Most folks thought prayer a pitiful weapon, but Hardie knew better. He'd grown up in the small town of Blackwell, Oklahoma. Back in the 1950s, people in rural Oklahoma were not only patriotic; they believed in prayer. Folks in Blackwell took care of their own.

When the first of their young men left home to fight the war in Korea, the townspeople decided to stop everything at noon each day and pray for one minute, asking God to keep all their boys safe....

The shrill fire siren pierced the silence each day at noon. The whole town stopped; cars pulled to the side of the road while green lights swayed in the breeze; the barber stopped cutting hair; the beautician set down her hairspray. Business meetings at the bank fell silent. Waitresses stopped talking mid-sentence. Housewives bowed their heads over sinks full of sudsy dishes. The gas station attendant stopped pumping gas. Teachers in the classroom put down their chalk. For one minute, the residents of Blackwell, Oklahoma, prayed that their young men would come home alive and well.

Hardie had been a child when every single one of Blackwell's soldiers came home alive. He grew up hearing how people put aside their petty differences to pray in unity. Baptists and Pentecostals, Republicans and Democrats, those for the war and those opposed, all prayed in unity for one minute.

Unified Prayer

Hardie Higgins never doubted the power of unified prayer. As far as he was concerned, it was the most powerful weapon in God's armory—but one that people seldom used.

While waiting to be deployed, Hardie sat down and wrote the story of how Blackwell prayed their sons home alive. Handing out the story at a family support group meeting, he talked about the power of unified prayer. Families of the 130th Engineer Brigade decided to follow Blackwell's example.

They set their prayer time for 8 pm. A friend of one soldier in Kentucky stopped to pray at two o'clock in the afternoon, which was eight pm in Germany.

At eight o'clock, cell phones snapped shut, cars pulled off the road, dinners stopped being served, and everyone prayed for the brigade.

With the families praying in agreement, Hardie felt like their chances of survival had skyrocketed. But he didn't want to leave the entire prayer burden on the families. Somehow, he needed to get the brigade praying too. What could he suggest they pray? Hardie believed there was power in praying the words of Scripture, but which passage?

The Power of the Promise

Some people believed there was protection available when you prayed Psalm 91. Turning the pages of his Bible, Hardie read the passage. That was some promise, all right.

Is it possible, he mused, *for all the promises of the Bible to be activated the same way you activate salvation?*

According to the Bible, Jesus made salvation available for everyone when He died on the cross for our sins. Yet receiving salvation wasn't automatic. The Bible says that only those who believe with their heart and confess with their mouth that Jesus is Lord will be saved.

What if the promises of protection belong to those who believe in their heart and confess with their mouth that it is true? Might the way you access salvation be the way to access every promise in the Bible? If so, he would ask the soldiers of the brigade to pray and confess out loud the 91st Psalm each day.

Writing to a ministry, Hardie requested five hundred cards printed with Psalm 91. If he could get five hundred members of the 130th to pray in unity, it would be a powerful prayer.

When Hardie presented his idea to the troop, he was stunned to realize that five hundred copies wouldn't be enough. Most of the brigade, even those who didn't attend services, wanted to pray the psalm. Printing out more copies from his computer, Hardie helped the soldiers to personalize it:

The 130th Engineer Brigade dwells in the secret place of the Most High and abides under the shadow of the Almighty. The Brigade says of the Lord, "He is my refuge and my fortress; my God, in Him I will trust." Surely He shall deliver us from the snare of the fowler and from the perilous pestilence. He shall cover us with His feathers, and under His wings we shall take refuge; His truth shall be our shield and buckler. The 130th Brigade shall not be afraid of the terror by night, nor of the arrow that flies by day, nor of the pestilence that walks in darkness, nor of the destruction that lays waste at noonday. A thousand may fall at our side, and ten thousand at our right hand; but it shall not come near us. Only with our eyes shall we look, and see the reward of the wicked. Because the 130th Brigade has made the Lord, who is our refuge, even the Most High, our habitation, no evil shall befall us, nor shall any plague come near our dwelling; for He shall give His angels charge over the 130th Brigade, to keep us in all our ways. They shall bear us up in their hands, lest we dash our foot against a stone. The 130th Brigade shall tread upon the lion and the cobra, the young lion and the serpent we shall trample underfoot. "Because the 130th Brigade has set their love upon Me, therefore I will deliver them; I will set them on high, because they have known My name. The 130th Brigade shall call upon Me, and I will answer them; I will be with them in trouble; I will deliver them and honor them. With long life I will satisfy 130th Brigade, and show them My salvation.

Missile Attack

In Kuwait in February 2003, the brigade's most imminent danger was from Scud missiles. The surface to surface missiles had a thirty-mile range, explosive power, and could carry chemical or biological agents. Building bunkers in the desert, the 130th Brigade practiced huddling in them wearing flak vests, chemical suits, and gas masks. Soon the practices were over.

"There'll be no more alerts," the commander announced. "The next time you hear the warning siren, it will mean that a Scud missile has been launched and is heading toward us. When that happens, the men firing the Army's patriot missiles will have two minutes to identify it and, we hope, intercept it."

An ear-splitting siren sounded the alarm that a Scud missile was screaming its way to their coordinates. The fear was palpable as everyone ran for the bunkers.

"Be calm," Chaplain Higgins said. "Remember that we have protection from above, and I'm not just talking about patriot missiles. The only time you should worry is if you see me worrying. I'm not worried because we have lots of people praying for us."

A patriot missile streaked across the sky, hitting the Scud in flight. Drenched in sweat, the men left the bunker. The reprieve was short; at least two Scud missiles were launched against them daily.

Each and every one was intercepted.

Blind Spot

A month later, the 130th Engineer Brigade was sent into Iraq to build floating bridges over rivers to allow US troops to cross. Pressing deep into Iraq, the 130th was unprepared for what they encountered.

The road was lined with cheering Iraqi people, thanking them for their help.

As heartening as their welcome had been, each of them knew that Saddam Hussein's soldiers, and those sympathetic to his mission, were determined to kill them. Guns armed and ready, they slipped around the perimeter of an old chemical compound that had been a prison for Iraqi citizens. Inside, the cells were empty; no trace of the prisoners existed except for grocery bags stuffed with their identification cards. Hardie saw that men and women of every age had been held—and probably tortured—there. The identification cards were the only evidence that they'd ever existed.

"We're surrounded by the enemy!" a sentinel reported. As dusk fell, Chaplain Higgins found a blind spot in their security. *A mistake like that could cost all of us our lives!* For the first time, Hardie Higgins's heart pounded a rhythm so loud that he suspected the enemy could hear it.

Fear raced up and down his spine causing his mind to turn somersaults and his soul to lose its peace. *The Bible says that fear is a spirit,* Hardie reminded himself. *I've got to fight this spirit as though it were Osama bin Laden himself, because its every bit as dangerous.*

Fighting Fear

Hardie knew that the only way to fight fear and build faith was to meditate and confess the Word of God. For three hours, he walked the compound confessing Psalm 91. Finally, fear left, and faith surged to the surface. The Brigade finished the mission. Every soldier left the compound alive.

The next month, the desert sun beat down like heat on the Fourth of July on the 130th Brigade, camped north of Baghdad. A high-ranking visitor arrived. When it was time for the visitor to leave, a caravan of five vehicles escorted him to a plane.

They had no way of knowing that while they delivered their cargo, Iraqi insurgents crept onto an overpass and waited for their return with rocket-propelled grenades and machine guns.

The unsuspecting caravan saw nothing out of the ordinary as they approached the overpass. The first Humvee had just cleared it when machine gun fire erupted. A grenade hit the right taillight of one of the Humvees—but for some reason it didn't explode. Going 50 miles per hour, one of the drivers saw the grenade roll past.

Every third or fourth bullet was a tracer round, leaving a trail of light. Navigating through a shower of machine-gun fire, one of the drivers looked up and saw the tracer rounds form an arc over them. It looked like the caravan drove through a tunnel of divine protection, lit from above by the tracer lights.

Not a single person in the caravan was injured.

"I could see the bullet's trajectory through the tracer rounds," the driver explained to Chaplain Higgins. "It looked as though we were protected inside an invisible tunnel. I don't have any idea what it was."

Hardie Higgins knew what it was. It was the secret place of the Most High. *How long had they prayed and confessed that very Scripture over the Brigade?* So many soldiers had prayed it so many days he couldn't do the math.

The next morning, the Brigade commander, a strong and faithful man of God, walked with Chaplain Higgins to look at the vehicles that had been attacked by grenades and machine-gun fire. There wasn't a bullet hole in a single one of them. The only damage any of the vehicles suffered was a broken taillight. A new lens was screwed in place, and the damage was repaired.

Over time, the 130th Brigade grew to six thousand soldiers. Two of them suffered injuries, but not a single soldier was shot and not a single soldier died.

What are the odds?

Excellent, when you dwell in the secret place of the Most High.

Part Three

WHERE DANGER CANNOT REACH US

By Gina

Part Three

WHERE DANGER CANNOT REACH US

As encouraging as it is to read about God's protective power at work in other people's lives, what all of us really want to know is this: Can I be sure God will protect me and my family? Can I be certain He'll keep us safe in every situation?

In these perilous times, those are crucial questions and, thank God, according to the Bible, the answer to them is *Yes!*... and *No*.

Yes, God has promised to protect us from every earthly danger.

Yes, He is able to fulfill that promise in any situation.

Yes, He will keep us and our family safe 100 percent of the time.

But no, He cannot do it without our cooperation. He cannot guarantee the safety of even His own beloved children unless we live by faith in the security of His secret place.

As I learned years ago when I first grasped the revelation of Psalm 91, we don't automatically dwell in that place just because we're born again. It's not the default residence of everyone who is saved. The plain truth is, many dear, God-loving saints never find it on this side of heaven. As a result, some of them end up there early, their earthly lives cut short by some demonic danger because they never discovered God's promises of protection.

"How that can be?" someone might say. "How could God just stand by and let such tragedies happen?"

He didn't. He poured out His very life to stop them. He shed the blood of Jesus so that every person on earth could qualify for His divine protection and live under His sheltering wing. He included temporal as well as eternal safety in our divine covenant, gave us His written Word to reveal to us His protective promises, and sent the Holy Spirit to teach us how to walk in them.

God has done everything necessary to provide security and peace for us here and now as well as in the hereafter. With an intensity we cannot fathom, He desires to satisfy us with long life and show us His salvation. But He will not violate the divine operating principle of this dispensation to do so. He will not overturn His mandate: *"Now the just shall live by faith"* (Hebrews 10:38).

Faith is the unalterable foundation of this age of grace that Jesus ushered in two thousand years ago. The New Testament leaves no question about it: What grace provides, faith must receive—otherwise, God's gracious provisions do not benefit us at all.

As Christians, we have no problem understanding this when it comes to our eternal salvation. We know that the redemptive work of Jesus doesn't automatically save everybody on earth from sin. It becomes effective only in the lives of those who receive it by faith.

We accept that fact with ease, but sometimes it irks us when the same principle is applied to temporal areas, such as divine protection. We are tempted to get snappy at the suggestion that we, as individuals, are in any way responsible for cultivating and releasing our faith for those things. "God is sovereign," we argue, "He'll do whatever He wants in my life. If it's His will for me to suffer calamity or die young, then there's nothing I can do about it. If it's His will to preserve me to a ripe old age, that's what will happen. My future is in His hands."

Of course, we'd never want a sinner to adopt that attitude toward the eternal side of redemption. We'd be concerned if a lost person said, "God is sovereign. If it's His will for me to go to hell, there's nothing I can do about it. If it's His will for me to go to heaven, then I guess I'll end up there."

Because we understand how the new birth is received, we would feel obligated to correct such an unscriptural perspective. "No!" we'd say. "That's not the way it works. God sent Jesus to the cross to atone for your sins and secure your salvation. He has already made His will known by saying He desires all men to be saved. The next step is up to you. You must believe in His saving power. You must follow the directions in the Bible by confessing with your mouth that Jesus is Lord and believing in your heart that God has raised Him from the dead. *'For with the heart one believes unto righteousness, and with the mouth confession is made unto salvation'* (Romans 10:10)."

Unbelievers who don't understand God's ways are often incensed by that concept. They think it's unwise or even unkind of Him to give people the responsibility of choosing their own eternal destination. After all, some people might end up going to hell just because they neglected to pay attention to God's Word! Others might put off believing in Jesus until one day they died and it was too late! Such are the protests of those who reject the gospel.

As believers, we aren't swayed by such arguments. We realize that God created us all with free will, and there's no way around it: with free will comes responsibility.

But here's the irony. Somewhere along the line, we got the impression that our responsibility ended with the new birth. We assumed that once we secured our place in heaven by believing in Jesus as our eternal Savior, our faith job was done and whatever else happened to us was up to Him.

But that's not the way God's redemptive plan works. At least, not according to the New Testament. It says that in this age of grace and faith, God does for us what we believe He will do.

+ If we believe He forgives us and sets us free from sin, He does that for us. He says to us as He did to the sinner in Jesus' day, *"Your faith has saved you. Go in peace"* (Luke 7:50).

+ If we believe He bore our sicknesses and carried our diseases, He heals us and says, *"According to your faith let it be to you"* (Matthew 9:29).

+ If we believe He delivers us from the power of the devil, He says to us as He said to the woman with the demon-possessed daughter, *"Great is your faith! Let it be to you as you desire"* (Matthew 15:28).

+ If we believe He will keep us secure amid in the perils of life, He protects us as He did His first disciples and says, *"Nothing shall by any means hurt you"* (Luke 10:19).

Jump Off Job's Bandwagon

The Bible leaves no doubt about it—all God's promises are activated by the power of faith. They become real in our lives when we believe them with our heart and confess them with our mouth.

So it's no surprise that, according to Psalm 91, if we're abiding in the secret place of the Most High, we'll not only be trusting in the protection of God, but we'll be talking about it too. We will open our mouths by faith and say of the Lord, *"He is my refuge and my fortress; my God, in Him I will trust"* (verse 2).

That's the kind of language used by those who abide in the secret place. When the subject of a flu pandemic comes up, they say, "Oh, I don't worry about that. God protects me from pestilence of every kind." When people around them are fretting about possible terror attacks, they say, "God is my refuge, and He said in Isaiah 54:14 that terror won't come near me."

Secret-place abiders don't say things like, "Well, you never know what might happen. Sometimes God gives, and sometimes He takes away. Blessed be the name of the Lord."

Granted, there are some phrases like that in the Bible, but they weren't spoken by God's covenant people. They didn't originate with born-again believers who had access to the plan of redemption and the promises of God's written Word. They were spoken by a man who had never heard of Jesus, a man who didn't even have access to the covenant of Abraham, a man who knew nothing about the existence of the devil and assumed every calamity came from the hand of God.

Job was the one who said, *"The Lord gave, and the Lord has taken away; blessed by the name of the Lord"* (Job 1:21). And though he said those words with sincerity and respect for God, they were inaccurate. Job misunderstood the calamities that had befallen him. The Bible makes that quite clear. But for the most part, we've missed the point of Job's story, so believers have been repeating his words (and perpetuating his misconception) ever since.

To abide in the secret place of the Most High and enjoy God's protection, we must jump off Job's bandwagon. We must start talking like New Testament saints who read and believe the Word of God. We must keep His covenant promises in our mouth. Instead of echoing Job, we should echo David in Psalm 121:

> The LORD is your keeper; the LORD is your shade at your right hand. The sun shall not strike you by day, nor the moon by night. The LORD shall preserve you from all evil; He shall preserve your soul. The LORD shall preserve your going out and your coming in from this time forth, and even forevermore. (verses 6–8)

According to Bible scholars, Job lived long before those words were written. He lived before there was any Bible at all. There's no scriptural record that he had any formal covenant with God. So we can cast aside the fear idea that what happened to Job could happen to us too.

We can rest assured that if we're standing in faith on the blood of Jesus and the Word of God, the devil can't get to us like he got to Job. The devil doesn't have the power to kill our kids, wreck our finances, or steal our health. Jesus took that power away from him through His death and resurrection. He disarmed the devil and all his demonic hordes. He made a public spectacle of them and triumphed over them. (See Colossians 2:15.)

"If that's the case, why is the book of Job in the Bible? What's the point?" you might ask.

It's meant to be a divine history lesson, and like all history lessons, some elements apply to us today, and others don't. Think in terms of secular history, and you'll see what I mean. Consider the historic lessons we can glean from the bombing of Pearl Harbor in World War II, for example. We all know we can learn a lot from studying that event. But to do so, we must determine what part of it relates to us today and what part doesn't. Otherwise, we'll get confused.

Think of the problems we would have if we believed every lesson from Pearl Harbor still applies. What havoc it could create in international relations if we clung to the conviction that, because of what happened there, the United States should never trust the nation of Japan.

During a time of war when Japan was on the opposing side, that piece of wisdom was relevant—but not today. Things are different now. New treaties have been established. Relationships have changed. These days, Japan is an ally of the United States. Japanese and US soldiers fight side by side in international peace-keeping situations. Americans enjoy driving Japanese cars, and the Japanese enjoy watching American movies. Our nations are at peace with each other.

If we worry about a Japanese attack when we think of Pearl Harbor, we have missed the point. We've overlooked the valid lessons it can teach us, such as: Never let down your guard in times of war. Always be vigilant. Anticipate the strategy of your enemies.

In the same way, when we draw the wrong conclusion from this historic lesson of Job, it wreaks havoc in our spiritual life. Our faith in God's protection is wrecked when we think the point of the story is that calamity can strike and harm even the righteous, and there's nothing we can do about it. Sure, that was true in Job's life. He didn't know about the devil's strategies. He had no idea that what he greatly feared would come upon him. And he certainly couldn't open his Bible to Psalm 91 to learn how to thwart the devil's plans with words of faith.

If he could have, he would. He said so himself. He longed for God's written Word and knew somehow that if he had it, it would be his deliverance. *"Oh, that the Almighty…had written a book!"* Job said. *"Surely I would carry it on my shoulder, and bind it on me like a crown; I would declare to Him the number of my steps; like a prince I would approach Him"* (Job 31:35–37).

I wonder what Job would say to us today when we leave our Bibles lying unopened on our nightstands and accept calamity as a blessing from God. I suspect he would lecture us about neglecting the privileges we have been given. He would explain how he had to muddle through without the advantages that we have. He would remind us—with great passion, no doubt—that things have changed since his day. We have a better covenant than he did. We have the complete written Word of God. We have the indwelling Holy Spirit to help us understand it. We not only know the devil exists, but we also have authority in the name of Jesus to resist him, and when we do, he flees from us.

By the time Job finished setting us straight, we would no more worry about suffering the same calamities he did than we would worry about kamikaze pilots dive-bombing us on the way to work tomorrow. We'd realize that page in history has been turned. Thank God, it's a new day!

We'd also come away from Job's lecture with a better grasp of the lessons God intended us to learn from his story, such as:

1. Never let circumstances you don't understand convince you that God sends calamities into the lives of His people.

2. Never add to the grief of suffering saints, like Job's friends did, by telling them God is punishing them for some unknown sin.

3. Never accuse God of injustice, as Job did toward the end of his sufferings, by claiming that God sometimes rewards our good works by sending bad things into our lives.

Those are some of the most important points made by the book of Job, and they are points most of us missed.

How do we know? Because again and again we hear Christians say things like, "Well, Saintly Sally was the godliest person I've ever known. She had more faith than any of us, and God didn't protect her from danger. He let her die young in an accident. So that must have been His will."

If you read Job's story from beginning to end, you'll see that he eventually drew that same conclusion. He decided that despite his pure and upright life, God in His sovereignty had chosen to inflict undeserved suffering on him. In other words, *"he justified himself rather than God"* (Job 32:2).

But, as we all know, there were some things about the situation that Job had no way of knowing. When God set him straight, Job acknowledged his mistake and said:

> *I know that You can do everything, and that no purpose of Yours can be withheld from You. You asked, "Who is this who hides counsel without knowledge?" Therefore I have uttered what I did not understand, things too wonderful for me, which I did not know.*   (Job 42:2–3)

Once Job received this revelation, repented of his wrong attitude toward God, and prayed for his friends, the Lord restored Job's losses. He gave him twice as much as he had before, and blessed his latter days more than his beginnings. What's more, biblical historians tell us Job's entire trial lasted only about six months.

Overall, Job did amazingly well for a man without a Bible!

Let's learn from him and apply the wisdom he gained. Let's remember that if we want to dwell in the secret place of the Most High, we must refuse to let negative circumstances shake our faith in God's promises of protection. We must be bold enough to believe that He is the God who can do everything and that no purpose of His can be withheld. If He purposes to protect those who trust Him to be their refuge and their fortress—and His Word confirms that He does—then nothing can stop Him from doing so. We can be confident that *"surely He shall deliver you from the snare of the fowler and from the perilous pestilence"* (Psalm 91:3).

Surely, He will deliver us! Not possibly. Not occasionally. But surely, without fail, in every time of trouble, He shall cover us with His feathers and give us refuge beneath His wings. His truth shall be our shield and buckler. We shall not be afraid of the terror by night, nor of the arrow that flies by day, nor of the pestilence that walks in darkness, nor of the destruction that lays waste at noonday. A thousand may fall at our side, and ten thousand at our right hand, but it shall not come near us.

"Why that sounds like arrogance!" someone might say. "How dare we claim that calamity can't come near us?"

We dare to claim it because the Bible says we can. Indeed, it says we must make that claim if we want to enjoy God's protection. Those scriptural declarations are our defense. They are the truths that shield us from the arrows of the wicked one. They are the buckler that makes us impervious to his attacks.

Although our declarations of God's divine protection may seem brash to others, we don't say them in arrogance. We confess them with gratitude and utter humility, knowing that we did nothing to deserve God's protection. We qualify for it only because Jesus bore our sins and made us righteous with His own righteousness. We know about it only because God was gracious enough to give us His written Word. And we have the wisdom to walk in it only by the power of the Holy Spirit.

"But how do we keep the experiences of others who somehow failed to receive that protection from shaking our faith?"

We do this by applying the lesson we learned from Job. We acknowledge there are hidden things about those situations that we don't know, and we stand firm on the truth we do know. We maintain unwavering confidence in the fact that God has promised perfect protection to those who dwell in the secret place, and He never fails to keep His Word.

Never.

Feeding Our Faith on the Word

Of course, maintaining unflinching faith in God's protection these days isn't a walk in the park. We're barraged with a constant stream of negative news. Reports of car wrecks, kidnappings, murders, suicide bombings, and other violent events abound. All we have to do is turn on the television or the radio, log onto the Internet, or walk into the local coffee shop to encounter bad-news preachers eager to propagate the message of fear.

How do we stay strong in faith in the midst of it all? By feeding our hearts with a constant diet of the Word of God and by meditating on God's ability to protect us until the devil's threats against us seem flimsy by comparison.

They are flimsy, you know. The Scriptures prove it. They reveal that God has a history of overwhelming the devil with supernatural power every time he concocts some diabolical scheme to destroy God's believing people.

The Bible even indicates that God enjoys doing that kind of thing. He takes pleasure in showing Himself strong on behalf of those whose hearts are turned toward Him. (See 2 Chronicles 16:9). His glory shines brightest when His people are facing impossible situations, when there seems to be no way out, when it looks like the devil is about to land his final blow and put them down for the count. Those are the times when He who sits in the heavens laughs at His enemy (and ours) and sends him running for cover like a whipped pup. (See Psalm 2:4.) Those are the times when God's glorious power pitches a tent and dwells over us, and the world gets to witness the mighty deliverance of God! (See 2 Corinthians 12:9 AMP.)

How thrilling it is to read the Bible and see just how many times God has worked miracles to protect His people! How good it is to study those scriptural stories and remind ourselves that, no matter what threat we as God's people may face, it's not we, but the devil who opposes us, who should be cowering in fear!

Consider just a few of the things God has done throughout history to protect His people:

+ He drowned the entire Egyptian army—Pharaoh, chariots, and all—in the Red Sea after splitting the waters and guiding the Israelites in safety to the other side. (See Exodus 14:13–31.)

+ He blinded an entire division of the great Syrian army, surrounded them with horses and chariots of divine fire, and sent them trailing like helpless children behind a single, unarmed prophet to become his prisoners of war. Then He terrified the rest of the enemy forces with the rumbling of invisible chariots and the thundering of unseen horses until they fled in terror. (See 2 Kings 5:18–23; 7:6–7.)

+ He gave a teenage shepherd named David such a bull's-eye aim and mighty arm that he killed a bloodthirsty, ten-foot-tall giant and routed the entire Philistine army with a single, faith-slung stone. (See 1 Samuel 17:50–53.)

+ He personally joined three Hebrew teenagers and walked with them in the fiery furnace, surrounding them with such protection that when they walked out of the flames they didn't even smell like smoke. (See Daniel 3:13–30).

+ He sent His angel to muzzle the hungry lions so that Daniel could spend the night with them in safety, proving to the king that the *"God of Daniel...delivers and rescues, and He works signs and wonders in heaven and on earth*" (Daniel 6:26–27). (See also verses 16–28.)

‣ He answered the prayers of the early church and delivered Peter from a death sentence by sending an angel to rid him of his prison chains, guide him past armed guards and locked iron gates, and set him free in the Jerusalem streets. (See Acts 12:5–10.)

‣ He saved not only the apostle Paul, but a ship full of sinners, from a deadly storm at sea and deposited the entire crew in safety on the shores of Malta without losing even one. (See Acts 27:14–44.)

Of course, that's just a short list. The Bible contains many more such miraculous rescues, and each one can encourage our faith. Each one can remind us that if God is for us, none can stand against us. We can conquer every foe and escape every danger once we know we have God on our side.

My friend Hugh Jordan demonstrated this fact a few years ago in a way that caught my attention and encouraged my faith much like these Bible stories do. He lived out his own David-and-Goliath kind of experience at eighty years old when an 18-wheeler came barreling his way and threatened to smash him.

He was driving my seventy-eight-year-old mother to church when the incident happened. They were bumping along on the chug-holed farm-to-market road they'd driven many times, chatting and enjoying the ride. About one hundred yards from the intersection where they usually turned left, Hugh stepped on the brake and stopped in the middle of the road for no apparent reason.

My mother described the scene to me later and said she stared at him, mystified. "Why are you stopping here?" she asked.

Hugh, a man who has walked so many years with the Lord that he obeys the promptings of the Spirit without even thinking about it, answered the question with a sheepish shrug of his shoulders and a shake of his silver-gray head. He didn't know why he'd stopped. Somehow he just knew he should.

Before he could say as much to my mother, the explanation roared over the hill ahead in the form of tractor-trailer rig rocketing toward them—*on their side of the road.* For a few shocking seconds, they stared, aghast, as the monster truck tilted and spit roadside gravel from under its wheels while the driver struggled to regain control. Paralyzed with surprise, they watched its wide chrome grin bear down upon them, threatening to swallow them up.

Then, in the blink of an eye, it was over. The big rig jerked to the right and swerved back to its own lane, flying past them in a flurry of Texas road dust.

Still unable to speak, Hugh swallowed the softball-sized lump in his throat and exchanged grateful glances with my mother. They both knew if he hadn't stopped when he did, they never would have made it to church that day. They would have been celebrating in heaven instead, while on earth wrecking crews and EMT teams sorted out the deadly mess left behind.

Practice Paying Attention

Of course, that story leaves us with one big question. How will God manage to protect us in situations like that if, unlike Hugh, we haven't developed the habit of hearing and obeying the promptings of His Spirit?

With great difficulty.

Many times He can still save our hides by maneuvering us from the outside or by calling a more attentive believer to pray for us and thwart the devil's plot on our behalf. But that's not the way He prefers to work. That's not His highest plan.

Our heavenly Father wants every one of His children to hear His voice and follow the leadings of His Spirit. That's why He has given each of us the equipment we need to stay in touch with Him. That's why He assures us in the New Testament that:

+ Those who belong to Jesus know His voice and follow Him and won't be led astray by a stranger. (John 10:3–5)

+ As His disciples, we know and recognize the leading of the Holy Spirit who lives within us. (John 14:17)

+ Our Helper, the Holy Spirit, will teach us everything we need to know. (John 14:26)

+ The Spirit will guide us into all truth. (John 16:13)

+ We who are the sons of God are led by His Spirit. (Romans 8:14)

+ We have the mind of Christ. (1 Corinthians 2:16)

+ He is working in us both to will and to do His good pleasure. (Philippians 2:13)

+ When we ask for wisdom, God gives us as much as we need for every situation. (James 1:5)

+ We have fellowship—close, intimate communion—with our heavenly Father and with His Son, Jesus Christ. (1 John 1:3)

With all those scriptural assurances, you'd think we'd never have any trouble hearing God's voice. Yet we all do at times.

Often that's because we haven't developed our ability to use the equipment God has given us. We haven't studied our biblical handbook enough to learn how to use our spiritual cell phone. We've let other things so captivate our attention that when it rings, we don't notice. Even God, in all His great power, has a hard time keeping us out of trouble when we ignore Him.

He will try, because He is ever merciful and gracious. He will speak to us by His Spirit to waken us from our spiritual lethargy. He will send ministers and exhorters to encourage us to spend time seeking Him and getting better-acquainted with His voice so that in times of crisis we'll hear it with ease. But if we don't pay attention, if our Bibles remain unopened on the coffee table, if we keep sleeping through our prayer times, if we don't bother to cultivate our relationship with the Lord, we won't be dwelling in the secret place when calamity strikes. And unless God can find an intercessor to help us out, we'll find ourselves trapped in the fowler's snare.

The book of Proverbs warns us about the cost of neglecting our spiritual development. It tells us in advance that if we don't pay attention to God's Word in times of peace, we will pay the price in times of peril. It says:

> *Wisdom calls aloud outside; she raises her voice in the open squares. She cries out in the chief concourses, at the openings of the gates in the city she speaks her words: "How long, you simple ones, will you love simplicity? For scorners delight in their scorning, and fools hate knowledge. Turn at my rebuke; surely I will pour out my spirit on you; I will make my words known to you. Because I have called and you refused, I have stretched out my hand and no one regarded, because you disdained all my counsel, and would have none of my rebuke, I also will laugh at your calamity; I will mock when your terror comes, when your terror comes like a storm, and your destruction comes like a whirlwind, when distress and anguish come upon you. Then they will call on me, but I will not answer; they will seek me diligently, but they will not find me. Because they hated knowledge and did not choose the fear of the LORD, they would have none of my counsel and despised my every rebuke. Therefore they shall eat the fruit of their own way, and*

*be filled to the full with their own fancies. For the turning away
of the simple will slay them, and the complacency of fools will
destroy them; but whoever listens to me will dwell safely, and
will be secure, without fear of evil."*   (Proverbs 1:20–33)

Thank God, as Christians, we don't qualify for the fullness of
that warning because no true Christian disdains all the counsel
of God. When we do stumble into disobedience and violate His
commands, the promise of 1 John 1:9 rushes to our aid: *"If we confess our sins, He is faithful and just to forgive us our sins and to cleanse
us from all unrighteousness."*

Because we are God's born-again children, God will always
receive us when we turn to Him by faith in the name and the blood
of Jesus. His door will always be open so that we can *"come boldly
to the throne of grace, that we may obtain mercy and find grace to help
in time of need"* (Hebrews 4:16).

Even so, the warning in Proverbs can save us trouble and pain.
If we'll heed it and develop our ability to hear and obey the Word
of the Lord, we'll be prepared when disaster takes a swipe at us.
If we'll practice seeking God and being sensitive to His leadings
while all seems well and we're cruising with ease down the highway
of life, when the 18-wheeler of calamity tries to run us down, we'll
know exactly when to stop.

The Electric Fence of Love

There's one more thing I must confess about my friend, Hugh.
He is one of the kindest people I have ever met. Love is the guiding
principle of his life. You don't have to know him long to figure that
out. All you have to do is walk into Eagle Mountain International
Church, where he serves as a greeter, see his shining blue eyes—
all crinkled from years of smiling at everybody—and feel the

114 Godʼs Power for Protection

gentleness of his touch as he pats your shoulder or shakes your hand as you pass by.

What do Hugh's loving ways have to do with the protection of God that surrounded him on the road that dangerous day?

Everything—because love helps keep us in the secret place of the Most High. The life of love is the safest place on earth.

One person who understood that fact better than most was the apostle John. He had such a revelation of love's protective power that when he was persecuted for the sake of the gospel, his enemies couldn't find a way to kill him. No doubt, John would have been willing to die for the sake of the gospel if God had asked him to do so. He had such a burning devotion to the Lord that he would have laid down his physical life for Him, like many of the other early apostles did, if that had been God's plan.

After all, martyrdom is not something a true disciple of the Lord Jesus Christ shuns. The Bible says that those who are persecuted for being Christians receive greater eternal rewards. (See Luke 6:22–23.) Some of God's strongest people of faith have wanted those rewards so much that they refused to accept deliverance from the suffering of persecution in order to obtain them. (See Hebrews 11:35.)

The apostle Paul had that kind of attitude. He said he was glad to pour out his life on the altar of sacrifice in the service of God, and he did end up dying a martyr's death. But he indicated that he and God—not the devil—were the ones who decided when the time for that was right. Paul didn't let the devil cut his life short and rob him of fruitful labor for God. Despite the devil's constant attempts to kill him, Paul chose to finish his earthly race. He made that clear when he wrote to the Philippians and said:

With all boldness, as always, so now also Christ will be mag-
nified in my body, whether by life or by death. For to me, to

live is Christ, and to die is gain. But if I live on in the flesh, this will mean fruit from my labor; yet what I shall choose I cannot tell. For I am hard pressed between the two, having a desire to depart and be with Christ, which is far better. Nevertheless to remain in the flesh is more needful for you. And being confident of this, I know that I shall remain and continue with you all for your progress and joy of faith, that your rejoicing for me may be more abundant in Jesus Christ by my coming to you again. (Philippians 1:20–26)

The apostle John had that same attitude. He was willing to suffer persecution for preaching the gospel—and he did. But he wasn't going to let the devil kill him unless his death would glorify God and advance His kingdom. As a result, some historians say he was even boiled in oil and came out unharmed. Talk about God's divine protection! John knew how to live in it.

We should pay particular attention to these words he wrote in 1 John 4:

Beloved, let us love one another, for love is of God; and everyone who loves is born of God and knows God. He who does not love does not know God, for God is love. In this the love of God was manifested toward us, that God has sent His only begotten Son into the world, that we might live through Him. In this is love, not that we loved God, but that He loved us and sent His Son to be the propitiation for our sins. Beloved, if God so loved us, we also ought to love one another. No one has seen God at any time. If we love one another, God abides in us, and His love has been perfected in us. By this we know that we abide in Him, and He in us, because He has given us of His Spirit. And we have seen and testify that the Father has sent the Son as Savior of the world. Whoever confesses that Jesus is the Son of God, God abides in him, and he in God.

And we have known and believed the love that God has for us. God is love, and he who abides in love abides in God, and God in him. (1 John 4:7–16)

According to that passage, we don't have to be rocket scientists to figure out how to stay in the secret place of God's protection. All we have to do is follow two simple instructions:

1. Believe in and confess Jesus, the Son of God, as our Lord and Savior.

2. Make love the guiding force of our lives.

If we'll do those two things, we'll always be able to hear God's voice and obey it. We'll be so entrenched in His protective presence that the devil will find it downright impossible to lay a destructive finger on us. I know that sounds like an extreme statement. But the apostle John—who ought to know—said it's true.

We know that whoever is born of God does not sin; but he who has been born of God keeps himself, and the wicked one does not touch him. (1 John 5:18)

"I just don't see how that could be possible!" somebody might say. "After all, the Bible says the devil is the god of this world. He is the prince of the power of the air. He has wiles and strategies and weapons. He is a dangerous foe."

That's true. But Jesus conquered him and gave us authority over him. So if we abide by faith in Jesus and keep the command of love, love's power will keep the devil at bay. It will surround us like a spiritual force field so that we can walk without fear in the midst of danger. We can stand with boldness against the demonic forces arrayed against us and put them on the run.

When we walk in love, we can have the kind of confidence my five-pound Yorkshire terrier, Gracie, used to have when she strutted through our guard-dog-infested neighborhood in New York. What a picture of fearlessness she was! Whenever I took her for a walk, she would stroll without flinching past barking, teeth-baring canines the size of ponies. If they came charging toward her across the lawns, she either ignored them altogether or exposed her tiny teeth to let them know she was ready to take them on if necessary.

Granted, Gracie's courage was not rooted in spiritual revelation. She wasn't trusting God. She was enjoying the benefits of the invisible electric fences that prevented the guard dogs from leaving their yards.

Although she didn't know the fences were there, she realized that for some mysterious reason, every dog in the neighborhood was afraid of her. She had figured out that as long as she stayed on the street side of the curb, those wicked dogs could not touch her.

There did come a day when Gracie made the mistake that most believers make at times. She abandoned her love walk and yielded to the bitterness she harbored toward Duke, our neighbor's Labrador. Duke made a routine of leaving his calling card on our lawn while Gracie watched, incensed, through the living room window. Over time, she developed such resentment toward him that one day when I took her for a walk, she lunged at him and ended up on the wrong side of the electric fence. Latching onto his jowl, she growled with all the ferocity her featherweight frame allowed and dangled from his face, swaying in the breeze like a wind chime.

If I hadn't overcome my astonishment before Duke did, Gracie would have become a Labrador's lunch that day. But I recovered from my shock with haste and, apologizing to Duke's wide-eyed owner, grabbed my dog from the very jaws of death.

How many times has God done for us what I had to do for Gracie that day? How often has He had to rescue us because we got into strife, jumped to the wrong side of love's protective fence, and ignored the warning in James 3:16 KJV: *"For where envying and strife is, there is confusion and every evil work"*?

More times than we'd like to admit, no doubt.

It's a good thing God is gracious and merciful. If He wasn't, none of us have survived this long. Even so, we should beware of duplicating Gracie's mistake. We should learn to look the other way when our neighbor offends us. We should practice forgiving and living in love. Otherwise, we'll end up getting in strife and doing something stupid. When we do, unless an intercessor intervenes, the devil may decide to have us for lunch.

Keeping Our Eyes on Jesus

After all that's been said about God's promise of protection, if we're still not sure how it works, there's one sure to way to find out. We can look unto Jesus, the author and finisher of our faith. (See Hebrews 12:2.)

When it comes to living out the protective promises of Psalm 91, Jesus Himself is the ultimate example. During His life on earth, He lifted those promises from the pages of the Bible and personified them. He became a three-dimensional, flesh-and-blood representation of them. In Him, *"the Word became flesh and dwelt among us, and we beheld His glory, the glory as of the only begotten of the Father, full of grace and truth"* (John 1:14).

Skeptics may claim that God's promises of protection aren't guaranteed. They may argue that He doesn't really offer the kind of perfect protection we've described in this book. They may come up with theories that seem valid and examples that bring questions to our minds. But Jesus answered those questions beyond any doubt. By living out Psalm 91, He showed us exactly what it means.

Jesus did live it, you know. He based His entire life on the written Word of God. He knew that Word, believed it, and acted on it every day. He meant it when He said, *"Man shall not live by bread alone, but by every word that proceeds from the mouth of God"* (Matthew 4:4).

If we want to know what happens to a person who walks by faith in the promises of Psalm 91, if we want to know what happens to danger when it comes after someone who dwells in the secret place of the Most High, all we have to do is look at Jesus. He showed us what it's like live in complete safety in the midst of a dangerous, sin-wracked world. He faced its perils—the terror by night, the violence that comes in the daytime, the pestilence that walks in the darkness, and the destruction that lays waste at noonday—and conquered them all. Then He said to believers of every generation, *"Follow Me"* (Luke 9:59).

Sometimes we get so familiar with the gospel accounts of Jesus' life that we forget the dangers He encountered. We take them for granted because He walked through them with such ease. We forget, for example, that when He first preached the gospel in Nazareth, His congregation responded with violence. Instead of thanking Him for His message, they got so mad that they *"rose up and thrust Him out of the city; and they led Him to the brow of the hill on which their city was built, that they might throw Him down over the cliff"* (Luke 4:29).

Those Nazarenes didn't just consider pushing Jesus to His death. They didn't just holler and wave their arms and threaten to pitch Him over that cliff. They put their plan into action. They physically grabbed Jesus, dragged Him to the precipice, and shoved Him to the edge.

A person of lesser faith might have questioned the reliability of Psalm 91 at that point. A skeptic might have said, "Okay, Lord, You must not have meant it when You said no evil would befall me. You must have been speaking metaphorically when You said I wouldn't dash My foot against a stone, because I'm about two inches from falling headlong into a whole bunch of them, and no angels have showed up yet."

But Jesus didn't say that kind of thing. He didn't let circumstances affect His faith. Unmoved by threats of the murderous mob, He kept believing God's Word. And *"passing through the midst of them, He went His way"* (Luke 4:30).

That's how Jesus defeated the destruction that lays waste at noonday.

He handled the terror that came by night in a similar manner. It showed up one evening in the form of violent storm that threatened to sink His boat and drown Him and His disciples. How embarrassing that incident must have been for the devil! There he was huffing and puffing, slapping huge waves over the side of Jesus' boat, howling like a hurricane, and he couldn't even wake Him up. Jesus was so unfazed by the devil's nighttime terror that He would have slept through the entire event if it hadn't been for His frightened disciples. When the boat started filling with water,

> ...*they awoke Him and said to Him, "Teacher, do You not care that we are perishing?" Then He arose and rebuked the wind, and said to the sea, "Peace, be still!" And the wind ceased and there was a great calm. But He said to them, "Why are you so fearful? How is it that you have no faith?"*
> (Mark 4:38–40)

Have you ever wondered how Jesus could say such a thing? After all, the disciples had never seen Him silence a storm. How were they to know it couldn't drown them? What was Jesus expecting them to believe?

He was expecting them to believe Psalm 91. They knew what it said. They knew it promised perfect protection to those who dwell in the secret place of the Most High, and they had the Son of the Most High sleeping in their boat. They should have known they were sailing in the safest place on earth.

But they didn't, so Jesus had to tame the terror by night Himself.

When Danger Bites the Dust

Jesus overcame the perilous pestilence too—not just once or twice, but thousands of times. He was often surrounded by multitudes of people with every kind of malady imaginable, and He never got sick. He was unafraid of even the most deadly and contagious diseases. When the leper came to Him and said, "Lord, if You are willing, You can make me clean," Jesus didn't step back and pray for him from a distance. He didn't rebuke the leper for getting too close and endangering the health of others. He did the unthinkable.

> *Jesus put out His hand and touched him, saying, "I am willing; be cleansed."*   (Matthew 8:3)

Can you imagine the gasps that must have rippled through the crowd of stunned bystanders as Jesus pressed His fingers against the leper's blanched, decaying skin? Can't you just see them averting their eyes from the gruesome sight of the man's flesh rotting off his fingers and toes, pressing their sleeves against their offended noses to block out the stench of living death?

Some of those who thronged around Jesus must have shuddered with fear and withdrawn from Him as He reached for the leper. After all, leprosy was so contagious and incurable that, by law, lepers were forced to keep their distance from others in the community. To touch one was to risk a slow, horrible death. Everybody was afraid to do it in those days.

Everybody except Jesus, that is. He wasn't afraid of leprosy or any other vile disease. He didn't have to be. He dwelled in the secret place of the Most High, so those diseases had no power over Him. They perished under the power of Jesus' touch.

Not only did diseases fall under His power, but armed soldiers did too. The gospel of John says that a detachment of the Roman army came with Judas to the garden of Gethsemane to arrest Jesus just before the crucifixion. They showed up with lanterns, torches, and weapons.

> *Jesus therefore, knowing all things that would come upon Him, went forward and said to them, "Whom are you seeking?" They answered Him, "Jesus of Nazareth." Jesus said to them, "I am He." And Judas, who betrayed Him, also stood with them. Now when He said to them, "I am He," they drew back and fell to the ground.*   (John 18:4–6)

That must have been a sight to see: an entire detachment of the fiercest military force on earth at that time converging with weapons drawn upon an unarmed preacher, then toppling like dominoes in the dirt. As they dusted themselves off and scrambled back to their feet, they must have been wondering what hit them.

They didn't know, but we do. Those soldiers had been stunned by God's mighty, protective covering. They were mowed down by the power of Psalm 91.

If Jesus hadn't chosen to go with them, the entire Roman army couldn't have captured Him. Legions of angels would have come on the scene to make sure of that. (See Matthew 26:53.) Because Jesus lived by faith in God's promises of protection, nothing and no one could hurt Him. In the end, His persecutors were able to crucify Him for only one reason: because He allowed them to do so. He chose to put Himself in their hands in order to carry out God's plan.

Even after Jesus was on the cross, the devil was unable to kill Him. According to the Bible, Jesus stayed alive long enough to make sure that all prophecy was fulfilled and God's will was accomplished there, then *"He said, 'It is finished!' And bowing His head, He gave up His spirit"* (John 19:30). Jesus didn't die because the devil killed Him. He chose to die in order to pay the penalty for our sins. He died because His heavenly Father asked Him to become our substitute.

In other words, Jesus died in obedience to the command of God—not at the hands of the devil.

Since He is our example of divine protection, Jesus wanted us to know that. He wanted to make sure we understood that no harm could overtake Him without His consent. That's why He said:

> *I lay down My life that I may take it again. No one takes it from Me, but I lay it down of Myself. I have power to lay it down, and I have power to take it again. This command I have received from My Father.*   (John 10:17–18)

"But that was Jesus!" you might say. "He could live with that kind of power because He's the Messiah, the divine Son of God."

Yes, that's who He is, but the Bible says that when He came to earth, He set aside the powers and privileges that belonged to Him as God. He lived as the Son of Man. He *"made Himself of no reputation, taking the form of a bondservant, and coming in the likeness of men"* (Philippians 2:7). *"In all things, He had to be made like His brethren, that He might be a merciful and faithful High Priest"* (Hebrews 2:17).

Jesus lived His entire life and fulfilled His ministry by walking in faith on the Word of God and operating under the anointing of the Holy Spirit. Amazing as it may seem, He lived just like we, as born-again believers, are called and equipped to live.

In the process, He showed us the kind of protection that belongs to those who dwell in the secret place of the Most High. He provided us with a perfect picture—a living, breathing demonstration—of the power of God's protection.

Can we really follow in His footsteps?

Yes, He assured us we can. He said,

Most assuredly...he who believes in Me, the works that I do he will do also; and greater works than these he will do, because I go to My Father. (John 14:12)

In these perilous times, His words and example provide us with a guarantee of safety that no one else can offer. They point the way to the place where danger cannot reach us: the secret place of the Most High God.

SCRIPTURES FOR
PROTECTION

against the Egyptians." Then the LORD said to Moses, "Stretch out your hand over the sea, that the waters may come back upon the Egyptians, on their chariots, and on their horsemen." And Moses stretched out his hand over the sea; and when the morning appeared, the sea returned to its full depth, while the Egyptians were fleeing into it. So the LORD overthrew the Egyptians in the midst of the sea. Then the waters returned and covered the chariots, the horsemen, and all the army of Pharaoh that came into the sea after them. Not so much as one of them remained. But the children of Israel had walked on dry land in the midst of the sea, and the waters were a wall to them on their right hand and on their left. So the LORD saved Israel that day out of the hand of the Egyptians, and Israel saw the Egyptians dead on the seashore. Thus Israel saw the great work which the LORD had done in Egypt; so the people feared the LORD, and believed the LORD and His servant Moses.   (Exodus 14:19–31)

Then Moses and the children of Israel sang this song to the LORD, and spoke, saying: "I will sing to the LORD, for He has triumphed gloriously! The horse and its rider He has thrown into the sea! The LORD is my strength and song, and He has become my salvation; He is my God, and I will praise Him; my father's God, and I will exalt Him. The LORD is a man of war; the LORD is His name. Pharaoh's chariots and his army He has cast into the sea; His chosen captains also are drowned in the Red Sea. The depths have covered them; they sank to the bottom like a stone. Your right hand, O LORD, has become glorious in power; Your right hand, O LORD, has dashed the enemy in pieces."   (Exodus 15:1–6)

If you walk in My statutes and keep My commandments, and perform them...I will give peace in the land, and you shall lie down, and none will make you afraid; I will rid the land of evil beasts, and the sword will not go through your land. You will chase your enemies, and they shall fall by the sword before you. Five of you shall chase a hundred, and a hundred of you shall put ten thousand to flight; your enemies shall fall by the sword before you. For I will look on you favorably and make you fruitful, multiply you and confirm My covenant with you.   (Leviticus 26:3, 6–9)

When you go to war in your land against the enemy who oppresses you, then you shall sound an alarm with the trumpets, and you will be remembered before the LORD your God, and you will be saved from your enemies.

(Numbers 10:9)

Do not rebel against the LORD, nor fear the people of the land, for they are our bread; their protection has departed from them, and the LORD is with us. Do not fear them.

(Numbers 14:9)

When you go out to battle against your enemies, and see horses and chariots and people more numerous than you, do not be afraid of them; for the LORD your God is with you, who brought you up from the land of Egypt. So it shall be, when you are on the verge of battle, that the priest shall approach and speak to the people. And he shall say to them, "Hear, O Israel: Today you are on the verge of battle with your enemies. Do not let your heart faint, do not be afraid, and do not tremble or be terrified because of them; for the LORD your God is He who goes with you, to fight for you against your enemies, to save you."

(Deuteronomy 20:1–4)

The eternal God is your refuge, and underneath are the everlasting arms; He will thrust out the enemy from before you, and will say, "Destroy!"   (Deuteronomy 33:27)

Happy are you, O Israel! Who is like you, a people saved by the LORD, the shield of your help and the sword of your majesty! Your enemies shall submit to you, and you shall tread down their high places.   (Deuteronomy 33:29)

No man shall be able to stand before you all the days of your life; as I was with Moses, so I will be with you. I will not leave you nor forsake you. Be strong and of good courage, for to this people you shall divide as an inheritance the land which I swore to their fathers to give them. Only be strong and very courageous, that you may observe to do according to all the law which Moses My servant commanded you; do not turn from it to the right hand or to the left, that you may prosper wherever you go. This Book of the Law shall not depart from your mouth, but you shall meditate in it day and night, that you may observe to do according to all that is written in it. For then you will make your way prosperous, and then you will have good success. Have I not commanded you? Be strong and of good courage; do not be afraid, nor be dismayed, for the LORD your God is with you wherever you go.   (Joshua 1:5–9)

So the LORD gave to Israel all the land of which He had sworn to give to their fathers, and they took possession of it and dwelt in it. The LORD gave them rest all around, according to all that He had sworn to their fathers. And not a man of all their enemies stood against them; the LORD delivered all their enemies into their hand. Not a word failed of any good thing which the LORD had spoken to the house of Israel. All came to pass.   (Joshua 21:43–45)

And the LORD said to Gideon, "The people who are with you are too many for Me to give the Midianites into their hands, lest Israel claim glory for itself against Me, saying, 'My own hand has saved me.'"   (Judges 7:2)

So the LORD saved Israel that day.   (1 Samuel 14:23)

Then all this assembly shall know that the LORD does not save with sword and spear; for the battle is the Lord's, and He will give you into our hands.   (1 Samuel 17:47)

Then David attacked them from twilight until the evening of the next day. Not a man of them escaped, except four hundred young men who rode on camels and fled. So David recovered all that the Amalekites had carried away, and David rescued his two wives. And nothing of theirs was lacking, either small or great, sons or daughters, spoil or anything which they had taken from them; David recovered all.   (1 Samuel 30:17–19)

The Lord is my rock and my fortress and my deliverer; the God of my strength, in whom I will trust; my shield and the horn of my salvation, my stronghold and my refuge; my Savior, You save me from violence. (2 Samuel 22:2–3)

I will call upon the LORD, who is worthy to be praised; so shall I be saved from my enemies.   (2 Samuel 22:4)

In my distress I called upon the LORD, and cried to my God; He heard my voice from His temple, and my cry entered His ears. Then the earth shook and trembled; the foundations of heaven quaked and were shaken, because He was angry. Smoke went up from His nostrils, and devouring fire from His mouth; coals were kindled by it. He bowed the heavens also, and came down with darkness under His feet. He rode upon a cherub, and flew; and He was seen upon the wings of the wind. He made darkness canopies around Him, dark waters and thick clouds of the skies. From the brightness before Him coals of fire were kindled. The LORD thundered from heaven, and the Most High uttered His voice. He sent out arrows and scattered them; lightning bolts, and He vanquished them. Then the channels of the sea were seen, the foundations of the world were uncovered, at the rebuke of the LORD, at the blast of the breath of His nostrils. He sent from above, He took me, He drew me out of many waters. He delivered me from my strong enemy, from those who hated me; for they were too strong for me.   (2 Samuel 22:7–18)

They confronted me in the day of my calamity, but the LORD was my support. He also brought me out into a broad place; He delivered me because He delighted in me.   (2 Samuel 22:19–20)

You will save the humble people; but Your eyes are on the haughty, that You may bring them down. (2 Samuel 22:28)

For You are my lamp, O LORD; the LORD shall enlighten my darkness. For by You I can run against a troop; by my God I can leap over a wall. As for God, His way is perfect; the word of the Lord is proven; He is a shield to all who trust in Him.   (2 Samuel 22:29–31)

God is my strength and power, and He makes my way perfect. He makes my feet like the feet of deer, and sets me on my high places. He teaches my hands to make war, so that my arms can bend a bow of bronze.   (2 Samuel 22:33–35)

You enlarged my path under me; so my feet did not slip. I have pursued my enemies and destroyed them; neither did I turn back again till they were destroyed. And I have destroyed them and wounded them, so that they could not rise; they have fallen under my feet. For You have armed me with strength for the battle; You have subdued under me those who rose against me. You have also given me the necks of my enemies, so that I destroyed those who hated me.   (2 Samuel 22:37–41)

It is God who avenges me, and subdues the people under me; delivers me from my enemies. You also lift me up above those who rise against me; You have delivered me from the violent man.   (2 Samuel 22:48–49)

So the LORD brought about a great victory.
                                            (1 Chronicles 11:14)

If disaster comes upon us; sword, judgment, pestilence, or famine; we will stand before this temple and in Your presence (for Your name is in this temple), and cry out to You in our affliction, and You will hear and save.
                                            (2 Chronicles 20:9)

Now all Judah, with their little ones, their wives, and their children, stood before the LORD. Then the Spirit of the LORD came upon Jahaziel the son of Zechariah, the son of Benaiah, the son of Jeiel, the son of Mattaniah, a

Levite of the sons of Asaph, in the midst of the assembly. And he said, "Listen, all you of Judah and you inhabitants of Jerusalem, and you, King Jehoshaphat! Thus says the LORD to you: 'Do not be afraid nor dismayed because of this great multitude, for the battle is not yours, but God's. Tomorrow go down against them. They will surely come up by the Ascent of Ziz, and you will find them at the end of the brook before the Wilderness of Jeruel. You will not need to fight in this battle. Position yourselves, stand still and see the salvation of the LORD, who is with you, O Judah and Jerusalem!' Do not fear or be dismayed; tomorrow go out against them, for the LORD is with you."

(2 Chronicles 20:13–17)

And the fear of God was on all the kingdoms of those countries when they heard that the LORD had fought against the enemies of Israel. Then the realm of Jehoshaphat was quiet, for his God gave him rest all around.

(2 Chronicles 20:29–30)

After these deeds of faithfulness, Sennacherib king of Assyria came and entered Judah; he encamped against the fortified cities, thinking to win them over to himself. And when Hezekiah saw that Sennacherib had come, and that his purpose was to make war against Jerusalem...Then he set military captains over the people, gathered them together to him in the open square of the city gate, and gave them encouragement, saying, "Be strong and courageous; do not be afraid nor dismayed before the king of Assyria, nor before all the multitude that is with him; for there are more with us than with him. With him is an arm of flesh; but with us is the LORD our God, to help us and to fight our battles." And the people were strengthened by the words of Hezekiah king of Judah. After this Sennacherib king of Assyria sent his servants to Jerusalem (but he and all the forces with him laid siege against Lachish), to Hezekiah king of Judah, and to all Judah who were in Jerusalem…Now because of this King Hezekiah and the prophet Isaiah, the son of Amoz, prayed and cried out to heaven. Then the LORD sent an angel who cut down every mighty man of valor, leader, and captain in the camp of the king of Assyria. So he returned shamefaced to his own land. And when he had gone into the temple of his god, some of his own offspring struck him down with the sword there. Thus the LORD saved Hezekiah and the inhabitants of Jerusalem from the hand of Sennacherib the king of Assyria, and from the hand of all others, and guided them on every side.   (2 Chronicles 32:1–2, 6–9, 20–22)

Therefore You delivered them into the hand of their enemies, who oppressed them; and in the time of their trouble, when they cried to You, You heard from heaven; and according to Your abundant mercies You gave them deliverers who saved them from the hand of their enemies.
(Nehemiah 9:27)

But He saves the needy from the sword, from the mouth of the mighty, and from their hand.   (Job 5:15)

Arise, O LORD; save me, O my God! For You have struck all my enemies on the cheekbone; You have broken the teeth of the ungodly.   (Psalm 3:7)

O LORD my God, in You I put my trust; save me from all those who persecute me; and deliver me.   (Psalm 7:1)

My defense is of God, who saves the upright in heart.

(Psalm 7:10)

The LORD also will be a refuge for the oppressed, a refuge in times of trouble.

(Psalm 9:9)

Show Your marvelous lovingkindness by Your right hand, O You who save those who trust in You from those who rise up against them.

(Psalm 17:7)

I will love You, O LORD, my strength. The LORD is my rock and my fortress and my deliverer; my God, my strength, in whom I will trust; my shield and the horn of my salvation, my stronghold. I will call upon the LORD, who is worthy to be praised; so shall I be saved from my enemies.

(Psalm 18:1–3)

"For the oppression of the poor, for the sighing of the needy, Now I will arise," says the LORD; "I will set him in the safety for which he yearns."

(Psalm 12:5)

I will call upon the LORD, who is worthy to be praised; so shall I be saved from my enemies.

(Psalm 18:3)

Now I know that the LORD saves His anointed; He will answer him from His holy heaven with the saving strength of His right hand. Some trust in chariots, and some in horses; but we will remember the name of the LORD our God. They have bowed down and fallen; but we have risen and stand upright.

(Psalm 20:6–8)

Yea, though I walk through the valley of the shadow of death, I will fear no evil; for You are with me; Your rod and

Your staff, they comfort me. You prepare a table before me in the presence of my enemies; You anoint my head with oil; my cup runs over. Surely goodness and mercy shall follow me all the days of my life; and I will dwell in the house of the LORD forever.   (Psalm 23:4–6)

In You, O LORD, I put my trust; let me never be ashamed; deliver me in Your righteousness. Bow down Your ear to me, deliver me speedily; be my rock of refuge, a fortress of defense to save me. For You are my rock and my fortress; therefore, for Your name's sake, lead me and guide me. Pull me out of the net which they have secretly laid for me, for You are my strength.   (Psalm 31:1–4)

No king is saved by the multitude of an army; a mighty man is not delivered by great strength. A horse is a vain hope for safety; neither shall it deliver any by its great strength. Behold, the eye of the LORD is on those who fear Him, on those who hope in His mercy, to deliver their soul from death, and to keep them alive in famine.
(Psalm 33:16–19)

This poor man cried out, and the LORD heard him, and saved him out of all his troubles. The angel of the Lord encamps all around those who fear Him, and delivers them.   (Psalm 34:6–7)

The LORD is near to those who have a broken heart, and saves such as have a contrite spirit. Many are the afflictions of the righteous, but the Lord delivers him out of them all. He guards all his bones; not one of them is broken.
(Psalm 34:18–20)

Rescue me from their destructions, my precious life from the lions.   (Psalm 35:17)

But the salvation of the righteous is from the LORD; He is their strength in the time of trouble. And the LORD shall help them and deliver them; He shall deliver them from the wicked, and save them, because they trust in Him.
(Psalm 37:39–40)

Blessed is he who considers the poor; the LORD will deliver him in time of trouble. The LORD will preserve him and keep him alive, and he will be blessed on the earth; You will not deliver him to the will of his enemies.
(Psalm 41:1–2)

For they did not gain possession of the land by their own sword, nor did their own arm save them; but it was Your right hand, Your arm, and the light of Your countenance, because You favored them.   (Psalm 44:3)

Through You we will push down our enemies; through Your name we will trample those who rise up against us. For I will not trust in my bow, nor shall my sword save me. But You have saved us from our enemies, and have put to shame those who hated us.   (Psalm 44:5–7)

God is our refuge and strength, a very present help in trouble.   (Psalm 46:1)

Call upon Me in the day of trouble; I will deliver you, and you shall glorify Me.   (Psalm 50:15)

As for me, I will call upon God, and the LORD shall save me.   (Psalm 55:16)

Be merciful to me, O God, be merciful to me! For my soul trusts in You; and in the shadow of Your wings I will make my refuge, until these calamities have passed by.

(Psalm 57:1)

He shall send from heaven and save me; He reproaches the one who would swallow me up. Selah God shall send forth His mercy and His truth.   (Psalm 57:3)

But I will sing of Your power; yes, I will sing aloud of Your mercy in the morning; for You have been my defense and refuge in the day of my trouble.   (Psalm 59:16)

Be my strong refuge, to which I may resort continually; You have given the commandment to save me, for You are my rock and my fortress.   (Psalm 71:3)

He will bring justice to the poor of the people; He will save the children of the needy, and will break in pieces the oppressor.   (Psalm 72:4)

He who dwells in the secret place of the Most High shall abide under the shadow of the Almighty. I will say of the LORD, "He is my refuge and my fortress; my God, in Him I will trust." Surely He shall deliver you from the snare of the fowler and from the perilous pestilence. He shall cover you with His feathers, and under His wings you shall take refuge; His truth shall be your shield and buckler. You shall not be afraid of the terror by night, nor of the arrow that flies by day, nor of the pestilence that walks in darkness, nor of the destruction that lays waste at noonday. A thousand may fall at your side, and ten thousand at your right hand; but it shall not come near you. Only with your eyes shall you look, and see the reward of the wicked. Because you have made the Lord, who is my refuge, even the Most High, your dwelling place, no evil shall befall you, nor shall any plague come near your dwelling; for He shall give His angels charge over you, to keep you in all your ways. In their hands they shall bear you up, lest you dash your foot against a stone. You shall tread upon the lion and the cobra, the young lion and the serpent you shall trample underfoot. "Because he has set his love upon Me, therefore I will deliver him; I will set him on high, because he has known My name. He shall call upon Me, and I will answer him; I will be with him in trouble; I will deliver him and honor him. With long life I will satisfy him, and show him My salvation." (Psalm 91)

Our fathers in Egypt did not understand Your wonders; they did not remember the multitude of Your mercies, but rebelled by the sea; the Red Sea. Nevertheless He saved them for His name's sake, that He might make His mighty power known. (Psalm 106:7–8)

He saved them from the hand of him who hated them, and redeemed them from the hand of the enemy.
(Psalm 106:10)

Then they cried out to the LORD in their trouble, and He saved them out of their distresses. He brought them out of darkness and the shadow of death, and broke their chains in pieces. (Psalm 107:13–14)

And rescued us from our enemies, for His mercy endures forever. (Psalm 136:24)

Though I walk in the midst of trouble, You will revive me; You will stretch out Your hand against the wrath of my enemies, and Your right hand will save me. The LORD will perfect that which concerns me; Your mercy, O LORD, endures forever; do not forsake the works of Your hands.

(Psalm 138:7–8)

Stretch out Your hand from above; rescue me and deliver me out of great waters, from the hand of foreigners.

(Psalm 144:7)

Rescue me and deliver me from the hand of foreigners, whose mouth speaks lying words, and whose right hand is a right hand of falsehood; that our sons may be as plants grown up in their youth; that our daughters may be as pillars, sculptured in palace style.　(Psalm 144:11–12)

He will fulfill the desire of those who fear Him; He also will hear their cry and save them.　(Psalm 145:19)

For the turning away of the simple will slay them, and the complacency of fools will destroy them; but whoever listens to me will dwell safely, and will be secure, without fear of evil.　(Proverbs 1:32–33)

Fear not, for I am with you; be not dismayed, for I am your God. I will strengthen you, yes, I will help you, I will uphold you with My righteous right hand. Behold, all those who were incensed against you shall be ashamed and disgraced; they shall be as nothing, and those who strive with you shall perish. You shall seek them and not find them; those who contended with you. Those who war against you shall be as nothing, as a nonexistent thing. For

I, the LORD your God, will hold your right hand, saying to you, "Fear not, I will help you." (Isaiah 41:10–13)

But thus says the LORD: "Even the captives of the mighty shall be taken away, and the prey of the terrible be delivered; for I will contend with him who contends with you, and I will save your children." (Isaiah 49:25)

In righteousness you shall be established; you shall be far from oppression, for you shall not fear; and from terror, for it shall not come near you. Indeed they shall surely assemble, but not because of Me. Whoever assembles against you shall fall for your sake....No weapon formed against you shall prosper, and every tongue which rises against you in judgment You shall condemn. This is the heritage of the servants of the LORD, and their righteousness is from Me," says the LORD. (Isaiah 54:14–15, 17)

Behold, the Lord's hand is not shortened, that it cannot save; nor His ear heavy, that it cannot hear. (Isaiah 59:1)

I will deliver you from the hand of the wicked, and I will redeem you from the grip of the terrible. (Jeremiah 15:21)

Then Nebuchadnezzar was full of fury, and the expression on his face changed toward Shadrach, Meshach, and Abed-Nego. He spoke and commanded that they heat the furnace seven times more than it was usually heated. And he commanded certain mighty men of valor who were in his army to bind Shadrach, Meshach, and Abed-Nego, and cast them into the burning fiery furnace. Then these men were bound in their coats, their trousers, their turbans, and their other garments, and were cast into the midst of the burning fiery furnace. Therefore, because the king's command was urgent, and the furnace exceedingly hot, the flame of the fire killed those men who took up Shadrach, Meshach, and Abed-Nego. And these three men, Shadrach, Meshach, and Abed-Nego, fell down bound into the midst of the burning fiery furnace. Then King Nebuchadnezzar was astonished; and he rose in haste and spoke, saying to his counselors, "Did we not cast three men bound into the midst of the fire?" They answered and said to the king, "True, O king." "Look!" he answered, "I see four men loose, walking in the midst of the fire; and they are not hurt, and the form of the fourth is like the Son of God." Then Nebuchadnezzar went near the mouth of the burning fiery furnace and spoke, saying, "Shadrach, Meshach, and Abed-Nego, servants of the Most High God, come out, and come here." Then Shadrach, Meshach, and Abed-Nego came from the midst of the fire. And the satraps, administrators, governors, and the king's counselors gathered together, and they saw these men on whose bodies the fire had no power; the hair of their head was not singed nor were their garments affected, and the smell of fire was not on them. Nebuchadnezzar spoke, saying, "Blessed be the God of Shadrach, Meshach, and Abed-Nego, who sent His Angel and delivered His servants who trusted in Him." (Daniel 3:19–28)

Then the king arose very early in the morning and went in haste to the den of lions. And when he came to the den, he cried out with a lamenting voice to Daniel. The king spoke, saying to Daniel, "Daniel, servant of the living God, has your God, whom you serve continually, been able to deliver you from the lions?" Then Daniel said to the king, "O king, live forever! My God sent His angel and shut the lions' mouths, so that they have not hurt me, because I was found innocent before Him; and also, O king, I have done no wrong before you." Then the king was exceedingly glad for him, and commanded that they should take Daniel up out of the den. So Daniel was taken up out of the den, and no injury whatever was found on him, because he believed in his God. And the king gave the command, and they brought those men who had accused Daniel, and they cast them into the den of lions; them, their children, and their wives; and the lions overpowered them, and broke all their bones in pieces before they ever came to the bottom of the den. Then King Darius wrote: To all peoples, nations, and languages that dwell in all the earth: Peace be multiplied to you. I make a decree that in every dominion of my kingdom men must tremble and fear before the God of Daniel. For He is the living God, and steadfast forever; His kingdom is the one which shall not be destroyed, and His dominion shall endure to the end. He delivers and rescues, and He works signs and wonders in heaven and on earth, who has delivered Daniel from the power of the lions.   (Daniel 6:19–27)

Blessed is the Lord God of Israel, for He has visited and redeemed His people, and has raised up a horn of salvation for us in the house of His servant David, as He spoke by the mouth of His holy prophets, who have been since the world began, that we should be saved from our enemies and from the hand of all who hate us, to perform the mercy promised to our fathers and to remember His holy covenant, the oath which He swore to our father Abraham: to grant us that we, being delivered from the hand of our enemies, might serve Him without fear, in holiness and righteousness before Him all the days of our life.   (Luke 1:68–75)

So all those in the synagogue, when they heard these things, were filled with wrath, and rose up and thrust Him [Jesus] out of the city; and they led Him to the brow of the hill on which their city was built, that they might throw Him down over the cliff. Then passing through the midst of them, He went His way.   (Luke 4:28–30)

Now it happened, on a certain day, that He got into a boat with His disciples. And He said to them, "Let us cross over to the other side of the lake." And they launched out. But as they sailed He fell asleep. And a windstorm came down on the lake, and they were filling with water, and were in jeopardy. And they came to Him and awoke Him, saying, "Master, Master, we are perishing!" Then He arose and rebuked the wind and the raging of the water. And they ceased, and there was a calm. But He said to them, "Where is your faith?"   (Luke 8:22–25)

Behold, I give you the authority to trample on serpents and scorpions, and over all the power of the enemy, and nothing shall by any means hurt you.   (Luke 10:19)

I am the door. If anyone enters by Me, he will be saved, and will go in and out and find pasture. The thief does not come except to steal, and to kill, and to destroy. I have come that they may have life, and that they may have it more abundantly.   (John 10:9–10)

As the Father knows Me, even so I know the Father; and I lay down My life for the sheep....Therefore My Father loves Me, because I lay down My life that I may take it again. No one takes it from Me, but I lay it down of Myself. I have power to lay it down, and I have power to take it

We know that whoever is born of God does not sin; but he who has been born of God keeps himself, and the wicked one does not touch him.   (1 John 5:18)

ABOUT THE AUTHORS

ABOUT THE AUTHORS

Melanie Hemry

A former intensive care nurse, Melanie Hemry traded in her stethoscope for a computer and now writes poignant true life stories, many of which are set in intensive care. A 1988 winner of the coveted *Guideposts* Writing Contest, Melanie's stories have warmed the hearts of readers around the world. She holds a bachelor of science in nursing from the University of Central Oklahoma and a master's degree in Practical Ministry from Wagner Leadership Institute in Colorado Springs. She is the author of *A Healing Touch*. Melanie and her husband, Ken, are the parents of two grown daughters, Heather and Lauren, and they reside in Edmond, Oklahoma.

She can be reached at www.melaniehemry.com.

Gina Lynnes

A writer by trade and a minister at heart, Gina Lynnes has been a Bible teacher and associate pastor since 1996, ministering especially on the subject of prayer in churches both in the Unites States and abroad. A recipient of the National Religious Broadcasters award for her writing of the *UpReach!* radio broadcast, she has been involved in Christian publishing for more than twenty years, working behind the scenes as a writer and editor for a number of international ministries. Gina and her husband founded Lynnes Ministries in 2001. They spend their time ministering in Colorado, where they now reside, and in churches across the country.

Gina can be reached at www.lynnesministries.com.